JUAN MATA

SUDDENLY A FOOTBALLER

JUAN MATA

SUDDENLY A FOOTBALLER

Reach **Sport**

Dedicated to all the kids who dream of becoming professional players – just like I did

Reach Sport

www.reachsport.com

Copyright © Juan Mata

Written with Begoña Pérez
and Philippe Auclair.

First published in Great Britain and Ireland in 2019 by
Reach Sport, 5 St Paul's Square, L3 9SJ.

www.reachsport.com
@reach_sport

Reach Sport is a part of Reach plc.
One Canada Square, Canary Wharf, London, E15 5AP.

1

Hardback ISBN: 978-1-910335-36-9.
Trade paperback ISBN: 978-1-910335-83-3.
eBook ISBN: 978-1-911613-08-4.

Photographic acknowledgements:
Juan Mata personal collection, PA Images, Getty Images, Reuters.
Every effort has been made to trace copyright.
Any oversight will be rectified in future editions.

Design and production by Reach Sport.

Printed and bound by CPI Group (UK) Ltd,
Croydon, CR0 4YY.

CONTENTS

WITH THANKS

"**J**uan, we are very close now. You must do the acknowledgements and we are nearly ready to go." This is the story of the book. The story of many people trying to make it work, and then myself. It is not like I didn't want to do it, it is just that I was (I am) full of doubts: *I don't quite like this paragraph, I am not really sure about this title . . . can we change this photo please?* And so on and so on. Many delays, many emails, many calls. Too much of everything but here we are published, a bit (a lot) later than expected. So yes, these acknowledgements are very important and necessary, because without all the people I am about to mention, the book would be still sailing aimlessly (and probably endlessly) on my sea of doubt.

Many thanks to Begoña Pérez for the early hard work, for the hours of conversations which resulted in the first major draft of the book manuscript. Thanks Begoña, and apologies, for listening to my voice for those long periods, for your understanding, dedication, and for doing one of the most important things: the 'kick-off'. Thanks also to translator Marc Joss for his hard work converting our original copy to English language.

Many thanks to Philippe Auclair, the 'Iniesta' of the writers. The great simplifier. Merci for your countless trips to Manchester, for your great stories and advice, for your patience and your book recommendations. Thank you also (and very much) for being a great link between the publishers, agent and me. Gracias for taking care of your 'old but hard working' computer, which scared us a few times by pretending that all our changes were

ACKNOWLEDGEMENTS

deleted, until the very end. Thanks for teaching me something that is key – although I am not always applying it here to these acknowledgements – thanks for the art of simplifying.

'Many thanks' does not sum up how grateful I am to Jonathan Harris for his contribution to this book. To be direct, his input was probably more important than mine. He didn't let me give up. He understood my silences, played the right notes, at the right moments, and was polite enough not to tell me to f*** off the many times I deserved it. Thank you Jonathan for being there for me, even during difficult personal moments for you. I really appreciate it. Good luck to your QPR team and see you for the next book.

Many thanks to Reach Sport, and especially to Steve Hanrahan and Paul Dove, for their understanding and belief that this project could finally be completed. Thanks, too, to Roy Gilfoyle and Richard Williamson. I really hope not every book creates as many headaches as this one.

And finally, to put the ball in the back of the net, thank you to everyone that is mentioned in any form in this book. Thanks to most of you for being part of my life, and others for being a source of inspiration, motivation and learning.

Special thanks to my parents Juan and Marta, my sister Paula, Mamel, my girlfriend Evelina, both my grandmothers Tita and Mamina, the rest of my family . . . and you, Manolo, the boss. It is a shame that I didn't finish this book in time for you to see it, but I always said that if at any time I wrote a book (who would have thought it when you took me to training so many times, eh?), there was no way I would finish without mentioning and thanking you at the end.

Juan Mata, 2019

BELIEVERS

'You can change your wife, your politics, your religion. But never, never can you change your favourite football team.' – Anon

May 6, 2014

'**G**uys, let's do the lap of honour as we usually do for the last game of the season.' I felt embarrassed. We had just beaten Hull 3-1 at home, but we knew that, whatever happened on the last day of the season, we'd finish no higher than seventh in the league. This was a very bad position to be in for a club like Manchester United.

Such a successful club, such a historic club, the most decorated of them all in domestic terms, isn't used to looking at the top of the table from below. But a huge hole, one that was pretty impossible to fill, had been left after the departure of Sir Alex Ferguson. Yet the supporters cheered us on our way round Old Trafford. They gave us a genuinely warm reception. I didn't expect it in the slightest.

The strongest feeling within me was that we owed a debt to these fans. I'd arrived half way through the campaign, but it didn't matter. Seeing the way they transformed that disappointment into hope for the season to come made me feel very emotional.

It was a moment that I'll never forget.

I was aware that the situation might have been different at some other clubs, where we might have been booed – or have done that 'lap of honour' in an empty stadium. That experience was key in understanding the very special bond Manchester United fans have with their club and the players who represent it. I'm not sure that would have happened at many other clubs, especially outside of England – but I'll come back to that . . .

Believing together

That moment in 2014 was made all the more special, even unique, by the fact that it was Ryan Giggs' final game before his retirement in front of the Old Trafford crowd that had chanted his name to the tune of Joy Division's 'Love Will Tear Us Apart' for so many years.

He had taken on the role of player-coach that season and I could see on his face just how disappointed he was to have gone through such a bad spell in terms of results, something he had barely experienced before in his long, long career.

He wasn't the only one. People like Rio Ferdinand, Nemanja Vidić and Patrice Evra, who had known such fantastic success with the club, were also trying to put on a brave face but did not always succeed.

After so many years, the Old Trafford crowd hadn't got

what it deserved, yet they still taught us a lesson in how to behave in adversity.

Once the match was over, I discussed with David de Gea and Rio Ferdinand just how incredible a scene I thought it had been. "That's what they're like here," they told me. "They've been key to this club's success. They understand that teams go through different stages, they know their football, their support is unconditional." The reaction that all these legends got was unforgettable. You could sense the love from every single fan at the stadium – one of those goosebump moments. They didn't deserve less. Neither did the crowd.

If there is something I have tried to cultivate for as long as I've been a professional football player it is to try and put myself in their situation, to try and maintain a close relationship with supporters. To believe together. When we lose, I feel bad for the team and for myself on a professional level, but also for them because they suffer and have to take the defeat back home with them. I know that their disappointment is just as acute as ours, if not, even more so. Pain is the price you pay for loyalty when you're a fan, something which I think is experienced in England to a greater degree than anywhere else.

The fans are the motor that keeps the clubs moving forward, the ones who will always be around, through thick and thin. During the time that I've been at Manchester United, there have been some tough seasons, yes, and I've witnessed how frustrated people have been. Yet I've also seen another side to their support, which is hardly ever talked about, but of course, also limited – patience. They come to every single game with their best attitude, to push us closer to the win.

You may wonder how much we notice the fans during games. Do we see their faces? Are we aware of their emotions? To what extent does their emotional intensity get through to us?

In all honesty, on the pitch, everything happens so quickly that you barely even have time to look at the ball so it's very tricky to really take stock of what's happening in the stands. But, of course, you feel it.

Off the pitch, however, I do recognise lots of fans. I became familiar with many supporters who always waited for us after matches in Valencia, London, and now Manchester, and a different relationship took hold in their case, a greater closeness and complicity. They loved it, and so did I.

Connecting people

There are many ways in which a fan and a player can connect – a relationship which works both ways – but one stands out as the most uplifting and beautiful of them all: the act of scoring a goal. Of all the joys which the game gives to those who play it and watch it, none is as intense, none takes over you as deeply and as completely.

All the pent-up energy you've stored inside you explodes in one instant. What's happening around you ceases to exist. The emotion clouds your mind, to the extent you can forget how and with whom you celebrated.

When I look at a photograph of us celebrating, I cannot help it, I like zooming in on the fans' faces; seeing their expressions of joy, the explosion of feelings. It becomes much more than a connection. It is a true communion. No stronger bond can be created between a player, his/her club and its fans.

I will remember it forever. I scored my very first goal for Manchester United on March 29, 2014, against Aston Villa, at Old Trafford, in front of the Stretford End. The perfect setting for a perfect moment. The ideal bond.

But such perfect moments do not happen every time you go on the pitch, and, to me, a player can have many other ways to connect with the people who will be there to support him/her, whatever the circumstances.

Club culture

Every time I have joined a new club, I have tried to immerse myself in its history.

I like to know what the fans have experienced: they were there in their seats before I joined their family and pulled on their jersey, and they will be there long after I've gone. They are the true custodians of our colours, the people who keep the faith alive, a faith you're called on to share for a few years of your life, but which was there in them from their very first game and will enrich their lives until their very last.

Whenever I set foot in a new dressing room, I try to open myself to what it means to the fans. I'll take in the photographs that line the corridors of the stadium and training ground. I'll read about the club's origins, its great and not-so-great times, its tragedies, who its great players have been and what they have achieved. And, if I can, I will spend some time in its museum, as I did at Mestalla, Stamford Bridge and Old Trafford.

To me, it's important not to only be a passer-by when you join a team. I'm wearing that shirt so what does it mean, what does it stand for? This is not a detail. This is a crucial part in building a sentiment of belonging, which, in turn, will feed your hunger to do well, to be worthy of playing your part in your club's history.

Storytellers

It is so much more enjoyable to discover clubs' histories through conversations and memories than by reading books or browsing on the internet, no doubt about that. There is a great solution for it, storytellers. Individuals that have been working in clubs for longer than anybody else and are always keen on telling great stories about the past. One of them is Bernardo España, whom we all called Españeta, the team's ever-present kitman at Valencia, a promising player whose career had been cut short by a motorbike accident when he was still a teenager, and who had devoted more than 40 years of his life to his beloved club.

He would tell me stories about legends like Kempes and Romario, but also Don Alfredo Di Stéfano, who managed the club on two occasions, making them Spanish champions and leading them to a win in the European Cup Winners' Cup. I remember also his little dog, 'Pocholo,' whom he always spoke about. Bear in mind that Bernardo is a public figure in Valencia; he still signs autographs whenever he goes out in the city . . . he is a star. Everybody loves him. People like Españeta are the living memory of a club.

At Manchester United, we have the wonderful Kath Phipps, an amazing lady who started working as the club receptionist at the training complex in the year the European Cup was won at Wembley, with Matt Busby, meaning she is this rarity in United's history: someone who managed to outlast Sir

Alex Ferguson, the witness to countless changes in our great club, a legend in her own right. Again, everyone loves her. How couldn't you? She is the best.

At Chelsea, we also had these special personalities around us . . . Alan and Frank (Frank Steer, the players' assistant, whom we affectionately called 'Bulldog' because of the faces he could pull). Both were ever-present in the dressing room. I am still in contact with them, exchanging messages here and there; they are very funny.

Again, these people make clubs great. The people behind the scenes, who are always there. To be honest, I really enjoy being surrounded by people who have been at the clubs longer than me, as I love to hear anecdotes from back in the day. I love asking questions.

When training finishes, I normally feel relaxed and am in no rush to get home, so, quite naturally, I enjoy striking up conversations with the people who work with us, whether that is a physio, kitman, chef (Mike the chef has some great stories from George Best's times!) . . . everyone.

Fan superpower

Maybe I feel this way because, deep down, I am also still a fan, a fan who has suffered a lot and who nearly lost his club – Real Oviedo, with which I'll always have a very special affinity, regardless of how I've come to love other clubs.

As every fan knows, suffering is a key part of what it is to support a team, and heaven knows we've had our share of suffering at Oviedo. As it's normal, I feel myself inextricably linked to that club's past, present and future, which is why, in 2012, when it was very close to going bankrupt, I did what many other fans did: I became a shareholder, along with other Asturian friends, Santi Cazorla, Michu and Adrián López. The club was saved at the last minute and the story had a happy ending: three years later, we got promoted to the Segunda División for the first time in 13 years. So, yes, I guess I know the emotions which run through the hearts and minds of the supporters who have shared their dreams with me.

That special connection, to me, is at the very heart of football: it *is* the very heart of football, if I think about it. That's why it can be so overwhelming when that bond is somehow cut.

Emotional goodbyes

A career is not just a succession of clubs and jerseys, but also of goodbyes. My farewells, one way or another, have always proven to be emotional moments for the fans and for me. It was very special at Valencia when I left the club after four fantastic years, having become close to so many people who had supported me throughout my spell there. There's even a peña valencianista Juan Mata, a Valencia CF supporters' club, which was founded by some family members, whom I adore. I've tried to keep in touch with the group over the years and they still put up the banner bearing my name at Mestalla. Crazy!

When I made the move, I really felt that I had to leave the fans a message, and not just take off without a peep. So, after passing my medical in London ahead of my move to Chelsea, I went back to Valencia to give a press conference and say goodbye to my team-mates, the manager and his staff, the workers at the Paterna training ground and the fans. Many supporters came to the training ground to show their appreciation, including, of course, members of the peña Juan Mata. It was an unforgettable experience, sad and happy at the same time. My father, (who, it's true, can be rather dramatic sometimes), claims that there hadn't been a farewell quite like it. Dads, eh . . .

On the other hand, and because of how the last days of the transfer were, I didn't really get the chance to say goodbye in person to fans at Chelsea, so I wrote a letter in my London flat the night before moving to Manchester . . . I needed to express my gratitude. It was all I could do. I wanted to feel comfortable within myself and with the way that I had changed clubs half way through the season. Those fans, who had voted for me as Player of the Year in back-to-back seasons, something which made me tremendously proud (overwhelmed, in fact), really deserved an explanation, or at least a goodbye.

We had won the Champions League, the Europa League and the FA Cup in those two years and other players could have easily picked up those awards, given the level at which the team had been performing, but they chose me. I will always be grateful to them.

A player can feel happy with his performances, goals and assists, but this happiness takes on another dimension when your own fans acknowledge them in the way only they can. That's also what happened when the Manchester United fans chose my bicycle kick at Anfield (2-1 to United, March 22 2015, not a date or a game that I'll forget any time soon) as the Goal of the Season, 2014-2015.

Again, fans. Again, grateful.

Back on old ground

For a modern professional football player, there is often a post-scriptum to their leaving a club: the homecoming, but in the 'wrong' shirt. It can be an unnerving, almost disorientating experience. You know the home dressing room better than the visitors', you set foot on a familiar playing surface, you bump into well-known faces and are set against supporters who used to cheer you on. Your body feels strange as an opposition player, particularly in the first few minutes of the warm-up (though once the whistle goes, there's no time left to process such emotions, and you automatically focus solely on the task at hand).

I had to wait more than a year to return to Stamford Bridge as a Red Devil on April 18, 2015. How the fans would react to seeing me in a Manchester United kit I couldn't predict. I thought it might also depend on how the game was going from Chelsea's point of view (they were three wins away from the title, and we had won seven games on the trot), but I quickly realised that supporters, English supporters especially, usually put the present to one side in order to show their gratitude to a footballer who played a big role at their club for a period of time.

It ended up being a fantastic experience for me. It always is when I play there. I didn't need to wait until the start of the game for the Blues fans to show me their appreciation. I felt genuinely emotional when I heard them applaud my name when it was announced over the tannoy during the warm-up and when I was substituted during the second half. It was the 70th minute of the game and I was getting ready to walk over to the sideline to be replaced by Adnan Januzaj. Suddenly everyone took to their feet and gave me a standing ovation. I will never, ever forget that moment. It completely surpassed my expectations.

The same thing had happened at Mestalla where I faced Valencia in the Champions League group stage in September 2011, after being a Chelsea player for less than a month. Their reaction was incredible. Also when, some time ago, we played there with United in the Champions League. I really feel at home whenever I go to Valencia. It is a great privilege to feel loved.

Kids are honest

Few things make me as proud as seeing a fan wearing a kit with my name on it. It still amazes me when I'm on the coach on the way to a ground and I see children with my name on their backs. It also gives me strength, especially when you come across a kid whose father tells you that you are his/her child's idol or that he/she has a poster of you up at home. I'm not exaggerating here: it is a genuine source of motivation and inspiration for me. Sometimes, it's enthusiastic children who are only starting to play football and the ball may even still be bigger than them.

A child's admiration is something special, as it is as pure as you can find, but it can be a similar story with older fans. I loved seeing how Upton Park paid homage to Mabel Rose Arnold, West Ham's oldest supporter at more than 100 years old, during the club's farewell celebrations at their old stadium. She had never missed a match at Upton Park since setting foot there for the first time, and the last one ever was against us. There, too, it is pure emotion.

'Sign for them, lads'

Because of all this, the importance of fans must be recognised not just in football, but in any sport. We, as players, must always try to find time to interact with them, something that isn't really difficult to do at the training ground or the stadium after a game . . .

There are always heaps of people waiting for us at Old Trafford when we come out of the tunnel on the way to our cars. I remember how one of our managers, Louis van Gaal, always insisted that we make time for them, and how nice it felt to listen to someone like him saying that. Sometimes, and it's understandable, you are in a rush and you simply cannot stop that day; others, the result hasn't gone your way and the first thing you want to do is get in your car and head home, lock yourself away in your own world and wait for the next game to come, But Louis van Gaal always told us:

"Boys, you know there are many people waiting outside. They want to see you irrespective of what's happened on the pitch. Now that you're heading to your cars, please try to stop and sign some autographs."

Of course, I know it's not that easy after a defeat, but is it easier for them? I don't think so . . . I find it a matter of respect, a matter of putting yourself in the others' position, an acknowledgement that the fans are the ones who make this sport so huge, after all. Louis was right.

Proud

Let me tell you a story which I think every professional footballer could tell you, something I've experienced on some occasions, and which goes something like this . . .

I'm muttering to myself. *I cannot believe I've missed that chance . . . why didn't I chip it over the goalkeeper?* I cannot stop thinking about it. We've just lost. One of the most important games of the season, we were playing at home and we couldn't get the three points. I'm incredibly frustrated. I get in the shower. No-one speaks. I get dressed and everyone is sad; some of the guys are clearly devastated. Defeat doesn't taste nice, not nice at all.

I leave the dressing room and meet family members and friends who've been waiting for me in the car park, but I'm not in the mood for anything. I drive back home, barely saying a word. I eat something, although I have no appetite. I go to bed. I can't sleep. I try to relax, but I can't. The night seems endless. The alarm goes off, and I'm not sure I've slept at all. I have to go to training, I put on the first tracksuit I see in the wardrobe, and drive to the training ground.

"Morning" is all that comes out of my mouth. I take the usual coffee, but I don't want to read anything, not even check the news on my phone, like I normally do. I feel horrible. I hate losing.

It is not the first time (it won't be the last) that I experience the feeling, but it always hurts the same, just as much, always. I do recovery training with the team, and we all start to encourage each other, thinking about the next game. It is what we have to do, as there is no time to feel sorry for ourselves, but that missed chance still annoys me.

I know that I need to get over it, somehow; so I continue with the recovery inside, with the physios and in the pool, until it's time to get ready to go home.

Monday goes by, but the feeling just won't go away. I don't

want to make any plans, I stay at home, I try to calm myself down and rest.

A late session is scheduled on Tuesday, so I get to the training ground at 3pm. I've had a late breakfast and a slightly better night's sleep. I speak a bit more with everyone, but I'm not in my best mood yet. The loss still smarts. The week goes by so very slowly, the anger is still there.

Recovery time again after training and I'm one of the last to leave the training ground.

My day, my week, is about to change, but I don't know it. It has been raining for a while, and it's very cold and dark outside. I get in my car and head home. Usually, there are fans outside the training ground, but after a defeat like this, and with this cold, you wouldn't expect anyone to be there. I see two people, plus the security guy, after the barrier. I slow down and stop. There is a man and a kid, both completely soaked. I open the window.

"C'mon man, we are with you, we need to keep going, let's go for the next game!" the kid says, "and about that chance, it doesn't matter, don't worry, you will score the next one! Keep going, stay strong, we are behind you!"

I instantly smile, say thank you very much, sign the kid's scarf, and drive away after thanking him for his kind words once again. Suddenly, I feel much better. A kid and his father have changed my mood. I cannot believe it. After the defeat, the disappointment, the sleepless night, the frustration, the tiredness.

How long have they been waiting? I ask myself. *How long did it take them to get here? They were soaked and freezing, it is unbelievable . . . that is true passion . . .*

Red traffic light, I stop, and these questions keep coming back into my head. And suddenly, I feel different. I feel motivated, encouraged, inspired.

I go home and tell everybody what happened. They had seen me so down over the last few days. "And how do you feel now?" they ask me after listening to the story. And all I want to say is: " Proud, very proud of them. Very proud to play for this club. Football without them is nothing."

They believe, they are the ones who travel to games to watch us, pay for a season ticket, pay for the kit and the souvenirs at the club's shop and buy the matchday programme. They make a huge effort, financial and emotional, in their lives to support us, an effort which deserves to be reciprocated.

We can do more in this respect, I'm sure of it. From my point of view, our responsibility goes beyond pleasing them by winning games. In fact, the best path to victory involves putting on a spectacle for the supporters that will be on playback in their heads when they get home. We have to give them reason to keep enjoying themselves.

Without fans, the game wouldn't deserve to be called 'beautiful'. Without you all, I would not be writing these lines.

2

THE TUNNEL

'The brave man is not he who does not feel afraid, but he who conquers that fear' – Nelson Mandela

A fierce sun was beating down on Oviedo on that July morning, yet I could feel cold sweat running over my whole body. I was sick with apprehension, scared as I had never been before. I was 15 years old and about to embark on a trip into the unknown.

The brief walk from the front door to my seat at the back of the car felt like it was taking forever. I put the luggage into the boot and I got in the car with my father, Juan senior. "Be good and take care of yourself!" were my mother Marta's words before she bid me farewell for good. It's something that she still regularly says to my sister and to me to this day, a decade and a half later.

"Relax, everything will be fine," both my mum and dad insisted. They must have guessed that I was having a tough time, despite my best efforts to conceal it.

We went from one end of the city to the other to pick up my friend Prosi and his father in San Lázaro, the neighbourhood where they lived. Prosi was the nickname that we gave Diego Álvarez Argüelles in the Real Oviedo youth academy – his blond locks made him look like the excellent Croatian player Robert Prosinečki, the legend who had played one season for our club in between stays at Real Madrid and Barcelona.

Our own Prosi was a classy and elegant midfielder with a hammer of a left foot, a powerful physique and fantastic vision. We were both improving fast and stood out in the Real Oviedo academy season after season. We had almost always been in the same team throughout our childhood – it had been Juventud Estadio before Real Oviedo – and worked our way up through the youth system in Asturias, forging a strong friendship along the way. We linked up very well on the pitch too, despite playing in different positions, as Prosi played in midfield and I was mainly a striker. The fact that we were both left-footed, if not one-footed, definitely brought us even closer together.

When we were 13 or 14 years old, rumours started doing the rounds at El Requexón, the Real Oviedo training ground, that scouts from top-level sides would be coming to watch us and were keeping tabs on our progress at their own academies. It was almost taken for granted that we would end up at a big club.

The reality is that every major Spanish club had scouts based in the north of Spain who would come to our matches every weekend. After months of tracking me, Real Madrid approached my family to arrange a trip to the capital to see their youth set-up.

I had offers from other clubs too, but the one that we found the most convincing was from 'Los Blancos'. The sporting and educational facilities were remarkable. The residence where I would live was inside the school and everything was very well structured. I was naturally quite impressed during our visit to the training ground, but also felt calm and confident when talking with the teachers at what would be my future school.

As a family, we ended up deciding that it was the best option for me in terms of continuing my education, while also training to try to become a footballer. The first big important decision of my life had being taken. It wasn't easy, of course, for my family (their little son was moving away) or for me (remember, I only was 15 years old), but I felt that gut feeling, that intuition, that conviction, that has always accompanied me on every major decision I've taken.

Prosi and his family also opted for Real Madrid. And so we found ourselves together again, as if it couldn't have happened any other way. Until that point, to us, clubs like Real Madrid, Barcelona, Atlético de Madrid and Valencia were on another level, even if we had faced them in several national youth tournaments. They might as well have been from another planet.

On the way to Madrid, a single idea kept swirling around my head: *It's unbelievable that we're going there. Do they really want to sign us? I don't know if we'll make the grade.* Prosi and I were feeling so tense – yet, in the front seats, our fathers were telling jokes and listening to music from the car radio, switching stations regularly, just as if we had gone on a day trip to the seaside.

It's true that my father is quite a joker, which always helps in tense moments. That was certainly one of them.

Trip into the unknown

When you leave Asturias and head to Madrid on the motorway, the most common route involves passing through the Negrón tunnel which links our region to the Meseta, the highlands of Castile and Léon. It's about four kilometres long. It's also a passage to another world.

Going through it raises feelings that are difficult to explain to someone who is unfamiliar with Asturias. In just a few minutes, you feel the sadness and nostalgia of a 'see you soon' or a definitive goodbye; when coming the other way, it is a warm feeling of happiness. You'll soon be back, your loved ones are nearby, this is home. That's why the Negrón means so much to the people from Asturias. That's why going through it sometimes feels so long . . . and others very short.

In this instance, the journey through the tunnel seemed to last an eternity, which made me an even bigger bundle of nerves than I already was.

Thinking back, it's a similar feeling to the fear that runs through you in the tunnel of the stadium before you go out on to the pitch. Every player suffers from that uncertainty. Some hide it better than others, but we all feel it. Thankfully, the anguish vanishes as soon as you enter the field of play and the game starts.

No matter how many times you walk through those tunnels in your career, you will still feel it – the fear, the nerves. I'll come back to that, but for now, let's continue with the trip to a new life . . .

Having made it through the Negrón, we all started to feel hungry and stopped off to eat in Valdemimbre, in the province of León. Prosi and I headed to the lavatory in the restaurant and I made the most of the brief moment that we had away from our fathers to confess my fear to my dear friend.

"I'm bloody nervous, so afraid," I told him.

"Me too," he admitted. "I'm shitting it."

That stop at the restaurant, that conversation with Prosi, are seared in my memory. Now, whenever I pass through Valdemimbre, I always remember that summer of 2003 and that car journey. Two teenagers were undergoing a crucial change in their respective lives.

Looking back, confessing to each other that we were terrified surely helped us endure the rest of the trip. In any case, as we approached Madrid and I started to see the city close up, and then when I discovered the facilities and saw my future team-mates and friends for the first time – the butterflies in my stomach were still there, but they belonged to a different species. The tension had gone. Excitement had taken its place.

It's like when a match that you're anxiously waiting for finally kicks off. If you are capable of transforming that fear to excitement, you are doing yourself a big favour.

I had previously visited Madrid on a school trip some years earlier, and the city had seemed huge to me. From the car, we were able to take in the Bernabéu, the enormous buildings on the Paseo de la Castellana, the theatres on Gran Vía and the general hustle and bustle of the town. *What sort of enormity is this?* I asked myself.

The residence and the school were not in the city, though,

as they were in the outskirts of Madrid, in an area called Villafranca del Castillo, which was the final stop on our long car journey.

Prosi and I said goodbye to our fathers and did the number one duty we had been assigned with: we phoned our mothers from the residence where we were staying. I don't remember being particularly anxious about not seeing my family at the time, possibly because I knew they would come to all the games every weekend. Knowing we would be reunited every seven or ten days dissipated my fears and inspired me to keep moving forward.

Starting from scratch

We met the head of the residence, Don Jaime, a very serious, disciplined and quick-tempered tall man with grey hair, who explained the timetable and rules to us.

We explored the building, the bathrooms, the games room, the dining hall and the bedrooms. We were full of excitement. I vividly remember the moment when I unpacked my suitcase and put everything in my new wardrobe. I didn't really know where to put my belongings because they'd always lived in the same place in my room in Oviedo. I had to find a new way to organise my things – an almost perfect metaphor for my new life. I had to start from scratch. It wouldn't be the last time.

The bedrooms were shared, with four beds that were separated into pairs by a big bookcase. Mine was the one closest to the window and Prosi's was next to mine. Two boys who were on trial occupied the other two. One was called Jordan, and the other was Kiko Insa, who now plays in

Malaysia, and has even become a Malaysian international as he was born in Kuala Lumpur. We were four kids sharing a room, chasing a shared dream.

It was definitely crucial to have Prosi by my side as someone I could confide in and chat to, especially in the tough moments. And I was there also for him. We really helped each other out from the first day and reassured each other whenever it was needed. I'll never forget those first few days, in which everything was new for me.

Soon enough, I started to get used to the group dynamics in the residence with my new classmates and team-mates. We were given a Real Madrid tracksuit and a school uniform which filled me with pride and confidence, and gave me a comforting sense of belonging. I got into a rhythm that meant I didn't spend too much time thinking about the huge change that I had gone through in my life, and could instead focus on what was happening here and now. I started to take things in my stride much more naturally. At times it felt like I was at an all-year-round summer camp with the discipline and timetables that come with it. The atmosphere was amazing, and I was truly happy.

We had to follow some routines which we gradually learnt to enjoy, like the bus journey from the residence to the training ground every afternoon after school. It was the last year that the academy and the first-team would spend at the old facilities on the Paseo de la Castellana.

Given the awful traffic at that time of the day, it would usually take us an hour and a half to get there, but we enjoyed it, or we learnt how to enjoy it. We were teenagers who had that school trip spirit and there was a constant mix of pranks, games and music towards the back of the bus – falling asleep with your mouth open, even momentarily, was a high-risk sport. Toothpaste, chewing gum, crisps or absolutely anything else would be used to decorate your face. You have to pass the time one way or another when you're 15 and stuck in gridlock, and we thought that this was the best way to do it.

We would train before heading back in the evening, having dinner and then we would have an hour of compulsory study at around 10 or 11, followed by bedtime. It may seem late, but given our timetable at training, it was the only slot when the teachers could be sure that we would hit the books.

At midnight, every bedroom light had to be switched off without fail. The smallest glimmer of light would result in the door bursting open with a guaranteed punishment to boot. That's how it was day after day.

A different adolescence

Our teenage years were vastly different from other people's, but the fact is that this didn't constitute a major sacrifice for the teenage me. I didn't really regret the fact that some 'normal' activities for a boy of my age were off-limits, such as going out with friends at the weekend, having a couple of drinks and so on. The most difficult part of this new life was not seeing my family for extended periods of time, but I managed to deal with it quite well, as if it were something which came completely naturally to me.

If I'm honest, I'd even say that I never spent much time agonising about it. It's true that I didn't have a normal adolescence – none of us could have had at the academy, no young footballer can – but I felt happy. I was playing football.

I was enjoying it. And I considered myself genuinely privileged (a feeling that has never left me, and which might explain why I've been able to deal with the ups and downs quite well), despite being hundreds of kilometres away from the people I loved the most. I had time for school, football and myself . . . I had no reason to complain. None at all.

I remember we would often go to Madrid whenever we had time off, and that meant normally Saturdays after the games or Sundays. Back then, going for a walk around the city centre was an epic mission. We had to catch the 626 or 627 bus in Villafranca towards Moncloa, which could really drag depending on the traffic. On arrival, we would then take the Circle Line on the Metro to the area that we fancied visiting.

Given that we had to be back at the residence by no later than 11pm, free time was worth its weight in gold. We would make the most of it by going to the cinema, bowling or other forms of entertainment in the early part of the evening. It also offered a chance for some family time if we had visitors. In other words, it was the best part of the week, alongside the matches themselves.

When we weren't up to heading for Madrid, in what we called 'lazy Sundays', we would walk around the meadows in Villafranca del Castillo, 'our place'. We would also go to Mocha Chica shopping area, where we'd visit the sweet shop and the great 'Ramonchu' burger joint. That's where we would watch the nine o'clock kick-offs, have a chat and eat dinner (what fantastic hamburgers he made!). A fabulous way to unwind before the week started all over again.

At that time, maybe I wasn't aware, or didn't want to be, of the rapid transformation that my life had undergone. It's only over time that I've realised just how significant leaving Oviedo at the age of 15 was.

It was the place where I had grown up, started kicking a ball around and made a fantastic group of friends (that I still have today) at Colegio Gesta. I moved away from my parents, my sister Paula – who is a very important person for me – my grandparents and the rest of my family. Until that point, I had always enjoyed football in my comfort zone at home, in Asturias.

Going to Madrid changed everything. My life started revolving around football, as if it were the star which had become the centre of my universe. I was at the mercy of the sport that I loved so much, from the school where I started studying, to the residence and my daily habits . . . it all changed and I was only 15. I've always tried, with some success I think, to adapt to every stage of my career in the best possible way. It is surely then, in those early days in Madrid, that I learnt how to do that.

The feeling of fear that came over me in the summer of 2003, especially when we went through the Negrón tunnel, was the first step on my path to becoming the footballer and the man that I am today.

It was a feeling that gradually disappeared during the first few training sessions. The unknown soon became familiar. Crucially, I realised that, despite my doubts, my level was similar to the others.

It also helped me improve, stay completely focused and give my very best. If I needed extra motivation and inspiration to move closer to my dream of becoming a footballer, I had it. I've got to be clear here: I had acquired 'it'.

I wasn't born ready

Nowadays, I hear many people say they were 'born ready'. I can understand why they say it . . . it sounds cool and strong. It has a ring of confidence and determination. It 'sells'. Well, I wasn't. In fact, I don't think anybody is really 'born ready', to become a footballer or anything else. I repeat, nobody is 'born ready'.

If anything, you become 'ready' along the way. But it is a process, not a gift that you are born with. You have to be ready, yes, and this is key, when the chance comes your way, but this is quite a different thing. In a way, we footballers spend our lives 'readying ourselves', before every game, because every game is a question, and you would be a fool to think you've always got the answer.

When silence speaks for itself

To illustrate this, let me come back to the beginning and take you to another tunnel; the tunnel in which the Spanish national team was waiting, before the match against Chile at the 2010 World Cup in South Africa, to take to the pitch. It was the third game of the group stage, a make-or-break game. We had lost our first match against Switzerland 0-1 and beaten Honduras, which meant the Chileans, who had won both their games, were topping the group and could send us home if we lost or even drew, should the Swiss beat the Hondurans.

On the way to the stadium, the team bus was like a moving block of ice. I don't remember feeling anything like that before a game. If you ask any player that was in that bus, they would tell you the same. Nobody said a word. You could feel the tension in the air. No music on the radio or the speakers. We were all listening to our own music through headphones. If you took them off, silence was all you could hear. *Fear.* So much was at stake; probably even more than what is at stake when you play for your club. A whole country was behind us, and we could have been crushed by the weight of responsibility. If we didn't qualify beyond the group stage, it would have a been a massive disaster for us.

It was then that Vicente del Bosque made one the greatest team talks I've ever heard. And he didn't use any patriotic messages, motivational language or anything like it. He only applied common sense. How he did it, I don't know, but he got the message across, and this message was not 'we will win, we will crush them, we're better, we have no right to lose' and so on, but – 'guys, if we lose, that's okay'. *What? What is he saying?* was the first thought that came through our minds.

He told us how, should that happen, time would heal the wounds, that it wouldn't matter in the long run, that defeat is a part of the game. And . . . that's it? Yes, that was it.

This sounds plain to you? Maybe it is, when I tell it like that. But del Bosque's genius was that he had judged the situation absolutely right, found the exact words that would make a difference. He played a big part in releasing that heavy tension out of our shoulders.

When nerves are good

We still had to play the game, however, and here is when that anecdote of the tunnel comes into the scene. I was heading to the bench with the other substitutes and wished all my team-mates good luck one by one along the way, as always.

When it came to the last player, Iker Casillas, I noticed that his face had turned unusually pale. "Are you okay, skipper?" I asked him.

"I'm shitting it, Mati," he responded with exasperation.

"Even at this stage, with all the games you've played and the World Cups you've played in, you're nervous? Come off it!" At that point, Iker had amassed more than a hundred international caps and won more trophies than almost any other footballer alive.

He nodded and said: "The day I'm not nervous is the day it's gone wrong, Mati."

Iker wasn't 'born ready' either.

3

NO RUSH

'Patience is bitter, but its fruit is sweet'
– Aristotle

Whenever I visit a school and young footballers ask me for advice (as if I was qualified to advise anything to anyone . . .), I always tell them: "Now is the time to enjoy it. Please, don't forget it."

They're at a stage of life when seeing football as a source of enjoyment has to be the priority, not being obsessed with competing or winning. Have fun, don't rush; it's not or shouldn't be about signing for big clubs too early or scoring tons of goals. Clearly defined targets do not really mean anything at that age, nor will they help you in the longer term.

Of far greater importance is building the values that are forged in the friendships and relationships you build with the people close to you: communication, respect and solidarity. Personal development is key, not naked or extreme 'ambition'.

These are not nice, empty words I use in order to say the nice, 'right' things. They are the foundation of everything

I believe in, be it inside or outside football, and had I not believed in them, I wouldn't be writing this right now.

That was the advice that I gave on one such occasion, to the children at La Fresneda. This was the place where I took my first steps as a footballer when I was five or six, under the guidance of Iñaki Artabe, a coach who was friends with my father, and was very knowledgeable about football. Much later, in the summer of 2015, when La Fresneda made me an honorary member, seeing the children's excited faces brought so many happy childhood memories flooding back.

Being seen as a kind of example always makes you proud, but it's also a responsibility to help youngsters understand that patience and perseverance are attributes which matter just as much in football as they do in life. You don't reach your goals by clicking your fingers. That's a fact.

Above all, although obviously sometimes it's difficult, you have to try to enjoy what you do, and take care never to lose that passion – what Vicente del Bosque used to call 'vicio'. Vicio for the ball, vicio for playing, vicio for football. It might sound like the English 'vice' – but is more something like 'appetite', 'desire for (enjoying)', 'need for (the ball)'.

Happiness versus relief

Looking back now, I am convinced that the crucial aspect in my own development has been this inner vicio for all these things and, most crucially, my vicio for sheer enjoyment. I love to play football so much.

There will be moments in a player's career – any player's career, mine included – when the demands of professional football are such that enjoyment is, at best, replaced by relief

– at playing okay, not losing, having won, 'having done your duty'.

When we win a game, or a trophy, of course there is an incredible feeling of happiness, but I would say that the predominant feeling is a different one if you play for a big club with high expectations: relief.

Johan Cruyff's message to his Barcelona players ahead of the European Cup final at Wembley in 1992 – 'Go out there and enjoy it' – was exactly what football should be about. But, sad as it may sound, enjoyment is not always on the cards.

After almost every game, I exchange messages with my good friend David Lombán, who plays for Málaga these days. The first question always is: "Did you enjoy it?" The answer is not always positive. How can you totally 'enjoy' a game when so much is at stake? It is very, very difficult.

I recall how another very good friend, Ander Herrera, is just before kick-off. Ander is terrified. The nerves, the fear, the tension . . . "not a nice feeling at all" he always tells me. Not being tense would be the unnatural reaction, when you think of it. If the great Iker Casillas is shitting himself before a game, what of Lombán, Ander or me? And we all have our own ways of dealing with it.

When he was at Athletic Bilbao, Ander told me that he used to dance around the dressing room and crack jokes to ease the tension. Some guys put music on – Ashley Young is our main MC at Old Trafford – others retreat into their bubble (normally with headphones on, playing games with their phone – yes, playing games on the phone, how life has changed, eh!).

We all have our ways to 'warm up in the head' – I can't

think of a better way to put it – to translate that tension into positive energy, or to just feel a little bit less worse, like Ander says. We are certainly away from the complete freedom of playing football with friends after school; and yet, had I lost sight of that feeling, I wouldn't have gone to the beautiful places where football took me in body and soul, I'm sure of that.

I was very lucky: I was never rushed. I owe this in no small measure to my parents, who both encouraged me to take pleasure in what I did without burdening me with unrealistic expectations and responsibilities, and never tried to rush me into anything related to football.

It's true that the idea of becoming a professional footballer did run through my head during my childhood; like every other boy, I had daydreams and fantasies about it, but that's all they were, and there was never any pressure from my family for me to make it as a player.

Dreaming of La Liga

The influence of having a footballing father didn't weigh me down either. In fact, I am going to tell you something that I have never told him: to me, setting myself the target of making my top-flight debut – without aspiring to much more – was more of a family challenge than anything else.

Why? Simply because, as a footballer, my father achieved promotion twice from the second division, once with Real Burgos, the other with Salamanca, but never got to play in La Liga, as he changed clubs each time, just before they hit the big time. So, if it never felt like my family was a burden, my father's influence was key from the outset nevertheless. I used to go to games and training sessions with him when he was a professional, and all that stays with you.

What I had in me was a determined personality, at times quite stubborn. It did bother me a lot and I would get very angry whenever we suffered a defeat or hadn't performed to our usual standard. However, and above all, I loved being outdoors, playing football or any other game. I wanted time to stop at those moments. I have that feeling stuck in my head.

The earliest football memory I have is of the house where we lived in Salamanca. I was around three at the time. I used to play with my sister with all kinds of balls, the kind of fluffy balls dogs play with, balls that weren't too hard – Mum's orders – so that we wouldn't damage the house. I already used my left foot in preference to the right, despite obviously not having a clue that there was a thing called 'football'. I might have possessed good co-ordination and motor skills, but, of course, it helps when you're born in the house of a footballer.

Football already conditioned my life back then. During my early years, we lived in Burgos, Salamanca and Cartagena – wherever my father's career took him. I suppose I already lived the kind of nomadic life that almost every professional footballer accepts as 'normality', and have never known any other kind.

Once we had settled in Oviedo, when I was five or six, I started playing in what you would call 'proper' teams, that is clubs with a degree of organisation and supervision by coaches, even if I was still too young to hold an official registration. As I've said, the first of these was La Fresneda, a huge sports complex with vast open 'praos' – playing fields – as we say in Asturias. Football was not just a game, a hobby or a passion, but also a means to socialise as a family at weekends.

As kids, we would play in tournaments everywhere, and after the games, all the families used to get together at an al fresco restaurant while we would keep playing football in the prao. We just wouldn't stop. It was fantastic, the highlight of the week. We were all friends and our families were as well. Football created a bond between us and our parents.

Oh, no . . . it's Sunday again

I was not a star pupil at Colegio Gesta 1, my primary school, but was diligent enough, the kind of pupil who doesn't cause too much trouble, enjoys the end-of-term trips to Madrid and Toledo, the B-grade student who picks up the odd A and C. As I remember it, the one blot in my life was Sundays. Sunday, the day when parents and grandparents checked on the homework (no laughing matter in my family), the day after the football game, the day before the first lesson of a long week. A horrible day, right?

That said, from a very young age, there was something almost sacred about studying and learning for me. My family played an obvious and big role in this. It was never about making a choice between the classroom and the football pitch. "Both can be combined for your benefit," they always told me, just like a professional footballer can combine life as an elite athlete with an appetite for discovery and self-development in other areas, whichever they may be; music, reading, travelling. Everything feeds off everything else. I guess it depends on everyone's personality. I'm just curious, and hungry. I always was, even then.

From La Fresneda to Juventud Estadio

In any case, school was also about football. What else do you do in a playground, I ask you?

One day (I was seven or eight at the time), my father came to pick me up after class. With him was a man with a big moustache.

"This is Laureano, your new coach at Juventud Estadio," my father said. "This is the club that I also played for. You will enjoy playing for him!" And this is how I started heading to El Cristo sport facilities to train twice a week, on Tuesdays and Thursdays.

We practised on a hard pitch that was supposedly 'indoor', but was actually open at both ends, then played our games on Saturdays at the Polideportivo El Cristo on a wooden surface. We later played on what was supposedly a grass pitch, but it was almost all sand and mud because of the constant rain in Asturias. Just so that you know that I'm not making this up, the average yearly rainfall in Oviedo is around 1,000mm – close to seven inches more than in Manchester. Yes, you read it right: *more*.

Although they might have been very wet, I have very fond memories of those early years at Juventud Estadio. I was now properly registered with the RFEF – the Spanish FA – and had my first taste of competitive football.

We even played in tournaments abroad. My first footballing trip outside of Spain was to a competition in Tarbes, in the south of France.

It was all new and fascinating. We spent a week there with our families and I still have photos from that adventure. The images are still fresh in my mind. We played on grassy esplanades, the rain poured down, the stands were soaked and the goals were just two poles stuck in the earth.

None of that mattered, because we had nothing to worry about. We just bonded, played, learned – enjoyed ourselves.

Juventud Estadio had a pretty decent side in my age group at the time. Prosi was there, as were Germán, Oscar, Santi, David, Roi, Iñaki, Javi; young boys still, but you could see they had it in them to maybe become professionals.

It doesn't mean that we swept aside every team that was put up against us, though. For some reason, we almost always came unstuck against our biggest rivals, Sporting Gijón, who dominated the youth championship in Asturias (we beat them once 4-0 with my dad as a 'manager' for the day – he always reminds me of that episode).

They had a fearsome player by the name of Cristian who scored more than 100 goals per season. Yes – 100! No wonder he was considered the best player in the region, along with Fran, a future team-mate of mine at Real Oviedo, who turned up for another Oviedo-based side called Astur CF, another of Juventud Estadio's big rivals. Fran, too, got to a century of goals in a single season. So, no, I was nowhere near the standout player of my generation. Even my dear team-mate Prosi stood out more than me because of his elegance on the pitch and his incredibly powerful left foot.

Wow . . . really? Real Oviedo!

I spent five seasons with Juventud Estadio, until I joined Real Oviedo at the age of 12. When I say, 'I joined', I don't think I convey what being accepted by Real meant for me at the time.

They were the big guys. Their shirt was the shirt everyone wanted to wear, my friends just as much as myself. This was a moment when I told myself, quietly: *Hey – maybe I'm not that bad a player!*

A career is made of a succession of forward and backward steps: this was a big one, and in the right direction. I'll be honest, it felt massive to me. Finally, I would be playing for Real Oviedo, one of the top two sides in Asturias, the other being Sporting. Both clubs had the reputation of having two of the best academies in the whole country, and deservedly so, which means the rivalry was ferocious at all levels, even more so for someone like me, who had always been a Real Oviedo fan.

I had jumped a level in one go, and not just in football, as I acquired a certain status within my group of friends. They started to address me as *el futbolista* – The Footballer – in the group. It's not just in football that people give each other nicknames; and this one stuck, for obvious reasons. Many years later, amongst the same friends, rocks on which I've built my life, I still feel that my place is in the group as *el futbolista*.

I could also see that at school, where the older students wanted me to play with them. They were in the same class as my older sister Paula, who was two years above me. They used to say to her: "Please, Paula, tell your brother to come and play with us." For obvious reasons, this made me a 'cool' guy, just because I played with the big boys. Looking back, what I didn't realise at the time was that this allowed me to improve my game, as I wasn't at the same stage of physical development as them: I had to think quicker.

No need and no reason for modesty at this time: I was a good player for my age.

What made me stand out, according to my father, was my knack for reading the game: I seemed to have an innate understanding of space and movement, a good first touch and a nice left foot.

While others ran after the ball, like most kids do, I held back and looked for different options. Later, I realised that I had always tried to think without the ball, in order to take quicker decisions once I got it.

I might not have had the same obvious impact as team-mates who were able to dribble past players with ease, but I did always get selected by the coaches, who could see that I could make the game flow.

My father didn't talk to me about my attributes at the time, though, which I imagine was down to the sound judgement that always informed my parents' attitude.

Another example of that thinking was that I could actually have moved to Oviedo earlier, when I was nine or ten, not 12; but they were convinced that it wasn't the best move if I wanted to develop as a player. Again, no rush.

They believed that I would benefit more from playing at more modest clubs, playing 'real football' – and suffer a little bit – on muddy pitches, which I think worked well for me.

I played football on surfaces where victories required a massive effort, rather than winning games 20-0 without breaking sweat at Oviedo. It was about ensuring that it wasn't all too easy for me at the beginning, learning from adversity and toughening me up, and for this, too, I am grateful to my family.

Thinking and playing

This has remained a key part of my game: trying to think as quickly as possible. *How can I give myself space? How can I create space for others?* Of course, I wanted the ball, I have *vicio* for the ball, but what's the point of having the ball if, suddenly, you're in the middle of three guys who are a head or two taller than you are?

So I would move into a pocket of space, and, when there was none, I had to think about creating it. When people say you've got 'time on the ball', if often means that, in fact, you've got the space to have the time. I learnt that very early on. Partly by instinct, partly as the result of a thought process. Football at every level, but especially in its highest form or expression, is about processing thousands of bits of information at incredible speed: it is played in the head. My managers at the time said that this was what made me different then: thinking while playing.

When you play, you have to keep your eyes, your ears and your mind open, because the game is talking to you all the time. It is the game which is telling us, 'do this', or 'do that'.

To me, the best footballers are those who always take the right decision, and I'm not just talking about pretty football, as many, even most decisions, are taken without the ball and it is the game which is the master: do what it dictates at this exact moment in time and you'll get your reward, with or without the ball. *Sprint or stop? Close that space or not? Anticipate that move or hold back? Tackle that player or wait? Risk the pass or kick the ball out? Shoot or cross? Dribble or pass?* Listen to the game, it will tell you.

The players I love to watch play are invariably those who do the right thing 99 times out of 100, and midfielders tend to do so more often.

In case you want some names, here you go: Messi (the midfielder, the winger, the striker, wherever he plays, he can do it all), Busquets, Kroos, Pirlo, Xavi, Xabi, Zidane, Modric, Iniesta (the great simplifier) . . . all these players have evolved in the process of understanding the game. Experience helps, naturally. It helps you solve situations which you have already encountered in a slightly different context, but which have a common thread running through.

I hadn't 'rationalised' that yet back then, obviously, about having a kickabout with the big boys in the playground. I wasn't talking about 'decision making' with my friends then. But I suppose I was raised that way, being a son of my father, a footballer, and a son of Spain, a country in which many clubs see it as their duty to teach the young how to use their heads as well as their feet: pass, move, and occupy spaces. The famous positional game.

Seeing from above

My awareness grew as I got older, when I started reading about it, and after I watched Zidane and Guti from the gods at the Bernabéu – I was 16 then – and wondered why what looked so clear to me from high up looked so confusing at pitch level.

I remember being at the top of the stadium, from where we couldn't almost distinguish the players, but I realised one thing. Yes, clearly, Guti moved where he had to, Zidane passed the ball where it had to go, but why weren't the others seeing it as they do? Of course, truly great players play as if they are seeing the game from above. I understood that something different was happening in their minds, but did I understand what that 'something different' was? Not really, not yet. It was a gradual process. It came with growing older, not just me, but also my friends, who started to ask different questions and tell me different things and opinions about the game. And it goes with the kind of football that I like, the one I am able to play, the one I have been coached to play, the one I loved and love watching.

Even then, as a young boy at Real Oviedo, I always knew what I liked or didn't like, but it's only later that I truly understood why. It might have been to do with how simple and easy things looked then.

Learning from the greats

Games tended to be extremely one-sided in our favour at the Real Oviedo academy, even at the age of 12. We would rack up huge scores: 10-0, 6-0, 7-0. Most of the teams in our league, barring Sporting of course, just couldn't cope with us.

And when this happens, the risk is to start believing you're rather good, when, in reality, you still have plenty to learn. Your game doesn't improve much by playing against opponents who do not have the same standards: in this context, it improves by training alongside your team-mates, where your level of competitiveness increases more than it does against inferior opposition.

The problem becomes how to gauge yourself outside of your own bubble; thankfully, we had the big youth football tournaments for that, like the Mediterranean International Cup in Catalonia, where we would come up against Real

Madrid and Barcelona. The giants. We felt that their players were taller, stronger and even better looking than we were. All they had to do was pull on those football shirts and that was that.

But it's not that we did badly in those tournaments, though. In fact, we realised that we weren't that far behind them after all. Before kick-off, we would go 'wow!' but not after we had left the pitch.

If you ask me, I've never been the type to idolise other players. I obviously appreciated and appreciate great players, and admire lots, but it's true that I didn't have a specific idol. That doesn't mean that I didn't try to learn from many, though.

I remember that, a few years later, it quickly became normal to be surrounded by 'legends' when I joined Real Madrid as a trainee. Emilio Butragueño trained the strikers, Michel took care of the wingers, Sanchis drilled the defenders, all of them fantastic players back in the day. I was gobsmacked when I saw what Guti and Robinho could do with the ball in training in one of my sessions with the first team, almost as if the whole thing was a joke, the backheels, the volleys, the no-look passes. Genius. A joy to watch. A joy to play with.

During those times (please forgive me as I'm jumping ahead in time here, but the memories run with excitement though my head as I write) we were sharing the pool and the spa of the training ground with the Galacticos, who had their own lift taking them from their dressing room to that level.

Every time we hear the lift, there's excitement among us. *Who will it be this time?* When it was Raúl, we knew he would talk to us, every time; the same went for Ivan Helguera – with whom I shared a room at Valencia four years later. Things move so fast. Things can be so difficult to process for a very young man. Will it be Casillas – with whom I enjoyed many moments together in the national team – or Beckham? How close and how far at the same time. How many of us will make it to the first team? To Primera División? We didn't know, probably not many, but hey, at that moment, we were sharing the recovery facilities with them, chatting with them, learning from them – and I can tell you, it felt more than enough.

Fabio Capello was the manager, and, along with five or six other members of the youth squad, I had been chosen to join the first team for a Champions League group game in Kiev*.

I didn't make the bench but I made the trip to Ukraine in the company of genuine legends of the game, Casillas, Ronaldo, Beckham – and Ruud van Nistelrooy, whom I sat next to on the plane. He did most of the talking, not that I minded, and made a deep impression on me.

"Keep doing what you do," he said, "keep your feet on the ground, believe in yourself." Such a short conversation that suddenly made me admire him even more than I already did. I will always remember his goals and celebrations at Old Trafford – now my home. Football is incredible.

Antonio Cassano was in the party too, and there is a great anecdote about him, let's say 'slightly different' to the one with Ruud.

On the day we arrived in Ukraine, we were driven from the team hotel to the Olympic Stadium to complete the final training session prior to the game. I was sitting in the front, Cassano was talking at the back. "I played in that stadium before with Roma," he said (Dynamo had beaten them 2-0 two years previously, when Cassano was the captain of that Roma team). And then, after he moved on to many different subjects – the girlfriends and the wild nights back in Italy – he acknowledged me and asked.

"Hey kid, what's your name?" he asked me.

"Mata," I replied.

"Well, Mata, listen carefully, if you want to be successful in football, don't do any of the things I just told you about!"

Antonio Cassano in his pure essence.

I could be me

If we speak about idols, my father loved – adored – Diego Maradona. He would play videos of Diego to me – another left-footer, you see and obviously I loved watching Diego, too. He was pure football: the control, the passes, the assists, the goals, the passion, the magic. An artist on a football pitch.

So whenever I'm asked about who my idols were, I always say my family. And it is not a cliché. My father had been a good pro himself and I loved listening to his football stories, wide-eyed, like any other boy.

As he was very sociable and knew many people in the football world, we met up with players like Roberto Carlos, Kluivert, Figo and Rivaldo at their hotel whenever they came to play in Asturias. It was crazy.

But my parents would always say that I should keep my feet on the ground if I wanted to become one of them one day: "If you want to stand out, you can do so on the pitch. You mustn't do anything forced off it. You have to be yourself and have personality." If you want to know where my incapacity for elaborate, choreographed goalscoring celebrations comes from, look no further. I will always be grateful to my parents for giving me the freedom to be myself. They 'let me be'.

What defined my childhood, football and family aside, was friendship and, in particular, the bond I formed with six other boys of my age. They were there before Real Oviedo and Real Madrid knocked on the door of the family home and they are still here today.

Each of us has taken a different career path: one is a lawyer, one is an engineer, one is an economist, one is a professional handball player and two work in tourism; to them, I am Juan and always will be.

Whenever I go to Asturias, or Madrid, where some of them live now, we meet up and catch up about our lives, about our problems, about our future. With them, as with my parents, the motto could be 'sin prisa' or 'no rush', just take it easy.

Haste is a bad counsellor

Although I was lucky because the way that my parents were, that was not a given. In fact, my mum and dad were the exception rather than the rule.

While at Oviedo, I could see how some parents told their children off at certain points of games, children who were at the peak of teenage vulnerability. "Why did you pass it? Why didn't you shoot? Why don't you do it all?" they'd ask.

There were parents who would position themselves behind the goal and spend the whole game shouting. Some of them wouldn't even hide their anger when the coach took their son off and they would scream from the sidelines: "This coach has no bloody idea! Don't take any notice of him, don't worry!"

I saw team-mates have to halt the game to beg their parents to zip it. There were players that actually hated it when their parents came and watched us. It was that bad.

When I was at Real Madrid, a player went so far as to interrupt a match to jump into the crowd to defend a father who had come to blows with someone. Yes, that embarrassing, that bad.

Thankfully, I never experienced anything of the kind myself. Those parents wanted their kids to be the best, to become professional or, yes, to earn good money at all costs. But they didn't realise that they were actually doing everything in their power to send their child's future in a completely different direction. They wanted to force things. They wanted to rush things.

We all can agree that excessive expectations generate less joy. That incessant demands can curtail your ability to enjoy the game. This is why my childhood was a time when football was a source of pure joy for me, free from the frustration that can be generated by excessive expectations, when success is seen as an obligation.

Winning or losing didn't matter as much then. In fact, some coaches rotated players constantly at the teams that I played for as a youngster. It was more of a formative process than a results-based one. And I completely agree with that. It's not normal for a ten-year-old never to get a kick of the ball because he or she might not be as good as others. The coaches tried to make changes, even at pivotal moments of the season, in order to try and improve each player, which I find admirable.

Whenever I've experienced difficult periods during my

career, I have always tried to recapture the essence of that stage of my life, in order to bring back that positive vibe. There's no better antidote than memories from a happy childhood almost entirely dedicated to the enjoyment of football. It isn't just about the advice that I gave to the children of La Fresneda when I visited them. It's advice I try to follow myself when things go really, really wrong. Go back to basics, Juan. Go back to the beginnings, when it was all about pleasure. When there was no rush.

There is another reason why I remember that particular game in Kiev. My sister really liked David Beckham and had asked me for his shirt. All embarrassing, of course, but I did as requested, and Beckham gave it to me at half-time (of course, he wouldn't remember now!). I asked him before the game and at half-time, when he entered the dressing room, he looked for me and gave it to me. Class. Who could imagine that the kid who asked him for his shirt that day would go on to play for the club of his heart? Not him for sure. Not even me.

4

JUDGEMENT DAY

'You can't connect the dots looking forward;
you can only connect them looking backward'
– Steve Jobs

Not everything happens by choice or force of will. When the opportunity to join Real Madrid at 15 arose, we had to make a big decision that would condition the rest of my life. Destiny had called. My parents, my sister and I had to sit down and discuss the pros and cons at length. It wasn't easy for them to let me go off to live in a different city, out of our comfort zone. There was a risk that it wouldn't work out. There was a risk that a crucial stage in my life, my teenage years, would be ruined.

My parents were aware of just how much I enjoyed my football, however, and were also reassured by the fact that the school at the Real Madrid academy was so committed to education. There was no danger of me dropping out. Knowing that there was a good structure in place in the capital to boost my personal development was key in their choice to leave the final decision with me.

Did I want to move to Madrid or not? Later on, they would tell me that my determination had made a big impression on them. "Yes, yes, no problem, I want to go," I insisted. My mother was unable to hide her worry, however. She, as is normal, was overcome by a feeling of uncertainty. Things could work out fine; but my life could also come off the rails. Thankfully, little by little, this feeling subsided and disappeared as she could see how well I had settled in at the residence alongside Prosi, and she got to know some of my team-mates' parents.

A similar structure was in place during international call-ups at youth level. Whenever we had to miss class because we had been selected, the Spanish Football Federation compensated by putting on complimentary lessons.

Ginés Meléndez, a key figure in Spanish youth football who supervised all age groups from Under-15 to Under-21, was entrusted with ensuring that our academic level didn't drop. So, if we played trial games in the morning, we would spend the afternoon in a classroom wearing our national team tracksuits. If it happened to be when we were studying equations in maths, for example, Ginés would give us an extra class on it. If we had to work on dictation, he would give us one to do.

This said, there were certain privileges at school, such as leaving class a bit earlier or jumping the queue at the lunch hall, both, occasionally, due to get to training on time. People who didn't know you well looked at you with some jealousy. I understood them. That was at school, and on the pitch, everybody wanted to beat Real Madrid.

Adaptation is key

We certainly didn't live in luxury, but the facilities were excellent, much better than is normally the case. I had team-mates, though, who systematically complained about everything: they didn't like the room, the bed, the schedule, the long bus journeys, the food, the teachers . . . They would sulk at any opportunity and never missed a chance to show they were unhappy (I'm sure you know someone like that). Most, if not all of them, didn't last long at La Fábrica. No surprise: such constant negativity ends up disrupting performances and is a waste of energy.

As for me, I was not one of these 'complainers'. I did not want to screw up the chance I had in front of me, I was aware of just how important that period was going to be if I wanted to make it as a footballer. I repeated to myself: *You've come to Madrid to try to play football, you're here to give your all to do well and enjoy all of it, so you don't have any regrets later on, whatever happens down the line.* I believe that having the capacity to adapt to my surroundings and different circumstances that have happened during my career, has undoubtedly been key.

The day

But, of course, it wasn't all rosy. Fear is one of the footballer's companions (as it is for human beings), and the worst of it was the fear of 'judgement day'.

There was a date marked in red in the calendar at the end of every season at Real Madrid. We would be told – one by one – if we were going to stay at the club or if we were 'invited to leave', either temporarily on loan, or for good.

We were all a bundle of nerves in the weeks leading up to that day of reckoning. I had the same feelings in my stomach – tension, anguish – that I still experience sometimes in the 'famous' tunnel, more often than not, and that I felt in the car on the way to Madrid to join La Fábrica. It didn't matter that I made it through the selection process on four occasions between the ages of 15 and 18: every time, I felt that wave of fear sweeping through me.

You can be fearful and be confident, however. What you fear is what you don't have control of. One thing I've learnt during my career is to try and focus on what's in your hands. Or in this case, in your feet. And forget what you cannot control.

If you think about it, it really makes no sense to let yourself be affected by things that escape your control, although it's obviously a difficult task to master. This is why the fears of 'not making the grade', on my arrival, as distinct from the fear of the process of 'judgement day' – would later decrease, although they would never 100 per cent disappear (at the end of the day, that was something that not entirely depended on me).

Things fell into place almost from the start. Prosi and I had arrived under the radar, something which also happened to me when I went to Valencia, but by the end of our first season, I was one of the standout players for Real's Under-16s, and I was promoted from the 'C' to the 'A' youth team within a year. I didn't put excessive pressure on myself, nor did I 'want it more' than others did. If my team-mates upped their level, I just did the same. It came to me naturally. I was adapting again. As a former team-mate at Oviedo, David Garmilla, once told me: "You have the ability to improve without making a fuss about it."

I didn't get carried away thinking about how 'good' maybe I was, but I knew that I must be doing something right. It is very important not to brag about what you've achieved, but to also know that you didn't achieve it just by chance, even if chance is perhaps the single most important thing when it comes to deciding a match.

At Real, I was playing with players a year and two years older than me and my performances at the 2006 Under-19 Euros in Poland saw me make the jump straight to Castilla, Real's reserve team, without passing through Real Madrid C, the club's third senior side which used to play in the Tercera División until 2015, when it was dissolved.

I scored four goals in that tournament, just one fewer than the tournament's Golden Boot winner, my Real Madrid Juvenil A team-mate Alberto Bueno. I had developed a great relationship on the pitch with Alberto, me playing as a support striker, just behind him, in our 4-4-1-1, be it with club or country. I've been told that some people still talk about our association in that team back in Madrid; the Mata-Bueno partnership. We had this kind of instinctive understanding of each other's game which makes it a joy to play as a pair.

In any case, it was all happening much faster than we would have expected, which was a good sign; but when 'judgement day' came, forget it! The apprehension was still there despite how well things were going on the pitch. The same process goes on at all academies, of course; but it's even more important at a club like Real Madrid because the effects of a rejection on a youngster whose life has been linked to a club of that stature can be devastating.

My parents and I would attend those formal meetings with the head of the academy and our coach, meetings which normally took place at the Santiago Bernabéu stadium to make it even more solemn and intimidating for youngsters like us.

They would evaluate how your studies were going and how you had been behaving over the past 12 months, before passing judgement on the footballing side of things. There were only two scenarios. Either you were going to join a certain team corresponding to your age group – oh, that feeling of relief – or you'd hear the words you dreaded to hear more than any others: "We're letting you go." Or "we believe that the best option for you is to go on loan". Or "unfortunately, the competition is high and you are free to go," or other such expressions designed to give a sweeter taste to the bitter pill. As if!

It's a huge blow for a 15 or 16-year-old to be told he isn't wanted any more. At that age, most teenagers are just concerned with the results of the year's final exams, but I don't think that even moments as stressful as these can compare with the selection process we had to endure as teenage footballers in Madrid. Our futures were at stake and we had put all our eggs in one basket (or so we thought). A few words, the wrong words, and your dream could be shattered – with no chance of piecing it back together (or so we thought, again).

Later, most of us would realise that there could be other chances, that not everything had hinged on that 'yes' or that 'no', and how important it was to keep believing in ourselves, even when it felt like no-one else around us did. But it sure didn't feel like that at the time.

I suppose you could argue that this process toughened us up, made us mentally stronger, regardless of the emotional impact on the day. It made us realise that football wasn't just fun, something to be enjoyed with friends, playing without a care in the world, as if there were no tomorrow. It was also about finding out whether or not you had what it took to fulfill a dream and make it your livelihood.

I should add that rejection doesn't automatically mean the end at such a young age, of course: some players simply develop later than others. But this one meeting was an emotional roller-coaster, something that a teenager cannot prepare himself for. I certainly couldn't.

I saw team-mates leave that room in floods of tears, with no other choice but to make plans to go back to their home town or join a different team. Some were so distraught that they even wanted to quit football altogether. That's why I believe it to be so important to tell (and constantly remind) all apprentices that a rejection does not have to be the end of the road. There has to be a back-up plan – the tide can change so quickly. It's a cliché but after one door closes, another does open. It just isn't worth beating yourself up about it. If someone doesn't have a positive opinion of you, it doesn't mean that you can't keep enjoying your profession. It's only your dedication, performances and passion for what you do that can turn that 'no' into a 'yes' in the not-so-distant future.

There are plenty of players who received a firm 'no' and who later managed to relaunch their careers and reach a high level. Jamie Vardy is one such example. Who would have thought that he would end up winning the Premier League with Leicester City when he had been released by Sheffield Wednesday when he was 16? That team which surprised the whole world (myself very much included) contained many players who had made the most of second chances in their careers. Danny Drinkwater came through the youth ranks at Manchester United, but never managed to break into the first-team. He was sent out on loan a number of times until settling at Leicester, where he became a key player and ended up claiming the league title that he probably dreamt of winning at Old Trafford when he was a youngster.

They are just two of hundreds of examples.

Plan B

The fact remains: they don't prepare you for failure in football. Most club academies focus on those who 'make it' and tend to forget about the others. This is something which frustrates, even angers me. It is just wrong. Would-be players should be told that not everything is going to go right all of the time, and, far too often, they are not.

The percentage of aspiring young footballers that end up making it as professionals is incredibly small. That is the truth, and, very important to remember. But as harsh as it sounds, that doesn't mean that it's impossible! It is possible of course, me and my team-mates are an example of it.

So it's always important to have a back-up plan. "Knowledge does not take any space," my mum used to say. And she is completely right. For all of the 99.9 per cent of children that play football and don't make it a living, you know what? It's fine. Life carries on. As long as you make sure that those who don't quite cut it, for whatever reason, don't feel that the world has ended. The clubs have a duty to tell the unlucky ones that, no, it is not the end of the world, and help them manage expectations and re-invent themselves; but how many clubs do? So few.

That must change. Life is more than football.

'Tell me who you're with, I'll tell you who you are'

The move to Real Madrid put my ability to adapt to new surroundings to the test for the first time in my life. And one important thing, something which you have control of, is knowing how to choose the company you keep. It helped that I was surrounded by genuinely fantastic people at Real Madrid, where so much was done to ensure that there was a healthy life balance between football and school.

When I was at the residence, I met players who were born in 1988, some of whom I'm still in regular touch with.

People such as Pedro Mosquera, who now plays for SD Huesca; Claudio Giráldez, top of the class, who played for some teams in Galicia as well as Atlético de Madrid B and is now a coach at the Celta de Vigo academy; the amazing Esteban Capelo, a Galician whom Pedro and myself roomed with; José Antonio Toto, our totico from Murcia; Samuel Sánchez Samu, 'Zami,' who later played for Málaga and other teams in Andalusia, another hard worker at school; funny Jonathan, 'Joni', who was from Motilla del Palancar in Cuenca. And Prosi, of course, our Prosi, who showed himself to be a really good student. I also met some great people in the older groups, such as Javi García, the Callejón brothers, Jose and Juanmi, Soldado, Rafa, Jurado, Casilla . . . I'd love us to be re-united at some point. We would have plenty of memories to talk about.

On the subject of friends, a quick aside: it is not always 'the easiest thing' to make friends with other footballers. Team-mates can be, and if we see it from this perspective, always are, 'somehow rivals'. You're competing against each other for a place in the side, after all.

There can be, as is human, jealousy, bitterness, a sense of real or imagined injustice. *Why pick him, not me?* For me, it all comes down to the way you behave, and above all, to be able to put your ego aside and realise that you are part of a team.

You should not lose your ambition to play, of course, but by doing that, you will probably feel better and you will probably play better when your turn comes. Managers that read this can confirm what I'm saying, although it is difficult to be able to always see it this way as a player because we all want to play every game, and we normally think we deserve to. We are funny, footballers, aren't we? I will develop this topic further in the 'Ego Trip' chapter.

We just have to remember that, in football as in life, it is impossible to be liked by everyone – but it's possible to be respected by everyone (your team-mates included, of course), as Sir Alex has said many times, and your behaviour is responsible for it.

Still, even if some things never change in a competitive environment, my feeling is that there was more 'normality' when I first discovered professional football than there is now; a greater sense of shared community within the dressing rooms. We spent less time in our own private worlds (smartphones, social media etc.) when we were together.

And with all this being said, it is thanks to football, of course, that I've come to meet amazing people and friends like Esteban Granero, Bruno Saltor, David Villa, Pablo Hernández, Oriol Romeu, Fernando Torres, Ander Herrera, David de Gea, obviously David Lombán, among others.

Funny enough, nowadays, I find it more difficult to relate to younger players than I do to some who are older than me – like Michael Carrick, for example, a wonderful, wonderful player I admire for his behaviour off the pitch as well as for his very special talent on it.

Michael: our quarterback

I'll allow myself another aside here if I may – I hope you're used to me moving from one thing to the next by now – as I'm writing this shortly after learning that Michael had decided to retire, and I feel it is as good a time as any to say how highly I think of one of his generation's best midfielders, not just in England, but anywhere in the world.

It astonishes me that he only got 34 caps to his name in an international career that started back in 2001 and only ended four years ago. I find it almost incomprehensible, when lesser players got called up twice as often or more to the England team.

You see, the style of a team changed – for the better – when it had a Carrick in it. He was a master of the pass, by which I don't refer to his accuracy in finding his team-mates (of course, he's extremely accurate!) but to his incredible gift in putting the ball exactly where and when you want to receive it, without breaking your movement. As if by magic, the ball arrives to the foot you want to use, in the space where you intended to run into, at the right pace, with the exact weight you require to make the best use of it.

He truly *gives* the ball, offers it to you. He's always looking to break the lines: all you've got to do is to give him the option, and he'll do the rest. In a millisecond, he'll have seen you, understood your intention, judged all the parameters and delivered the present to your door.

I guess that his art may be too subtle for people who prefer their football to be more obviously direct and laced with adrenalin. But he controlled games as very few others could, like a gridiron quarterback, especially in the 2012-13 season, when he was at his best, I think.

Players like him give rhythm and fluidity; they make you look good, too. Thank you for everything, Michael. Any kid who aspires to be a footballer should look up to you as a role model.

First setbacks: The learning process.

Now back to young Juan, who, as I said earlier, never thought he would play for Manchester United one day (not because he wouldn't want to, of course, but because it seemed impossible!).

In terms of my development as a player, of my technical and tactical understanding of the game, those years at Real Madrid were a defining moment in my career, the moment when the components of my game came together, the moment when I realised how important the balance between freedom and responsibility is on the football pitch.

Great teachers are those who know how to instruct you in both those 'disciplines' of football; and teaching freedom is probably the hardest of the two. Obviously, the instructions given by the coaches do matter a lot. Obviously, we had tactical and defensive duties to fulfil during our games. But it was great to hear coaches such as Carlos Salvachua, Trístan Celador, Alejandro Menendez, or Michel, tell us to be ourselves, to try things out, to let our instincts flow.

But not everything was always rosy at La Fabricá. There were moments of disappointment, as in the season when I made my debut with Castilla, Real Madrid's second team, at the age of 18, in 2006-07.

It seemed like I had enjoyed a positive period, scoring ten goals, when looked at from a purely personal point of view. But the story as a whole was a bittersweet one. We were relegated. It was a slap in the face, a wake-up call. We learnt that talent alone isn't enough.

There are plenty of experienced players in the second tier who may be less gifted than you, but they can beat you all the same. Which is what happened to us. It was a real eye-opener. But that would not be the only tough moment I experienced in Madrid . . .

Normally, I wasn't the kind of teenager who went through sudden, violent emotional swings. I had a stable personality. I could take things in my stride when they didn't go my way. I had ambitions, dreams even, but I didn't over-dramatise things. Except on one occasion. This is what happened.

I had been part of every Spain youth squad from the age of

15. As I mentioned, Ginés Meléndez liked the way I played and provided me with great support at the Spanish Football Federation.

This time, though, with Santisteban as a manager, I hadn't made the cut and would not take part in the play-offs to qualify for the Under-17 European Championships. That may sound unremarkable. Looking back, it surely was. But that hit me hard, really hard.

I was (and I am) very demanding with myself, and it didn't feel right that there were 'supposedly' many better players than me in Spain at my age. I couldn't understand it. How can this be possible? What am I doing wrong? I was very angry. And sad. This is one of the clearest images I've kept from that time in my life: crying uncontrollably in the showers at the Real Madrid residence.

I couldn't understand the reasons, I couldn't digest it. I hated that feeling so much I promised myself that I would do everything in my power to avoid having to experience it again. And I did. I wasn't left out of the national team for many years, until much later, at senior level.

And I didn't cry that time round.

5

DIFFERENT
ROADS

*'Do not judge people, you never know what kind
of battle they are fighting' – Anon*

"I can't quite believe what I'm signing, Juan." Sunny looked at the figures in his contract, astonished, and simply couldn't fathom it. Both of us joined Valencia on that day, July 19, 2007, after representing Spain at the 2007 Under-20 World Cup in Canada. We were on the verge of signing our first professional contract, but our journeys to reach that point couldn't have been more different.

'I will make you a football player'

Stephen Obayan Sunday, Sunny, was Nigerian-born and had endured very difficult circumstances during his childhood. He started playing football at school in his homeland and the game quickly became a means of survival, as is the case all too frequently on the African continent. But his story is not the usual one, or maybe, yes, unfortunately it is.

Sunny had no doubts about taking the plunge when an agent approached him at a tournament to offer him the escape path that he had dreamt of for so long: "Get the money together to pay for a flight to Paris, I'll be there waiting for you, and we'll turn you into a footballer in Europe." He didn't think twice. It was a blessing, he thought. He spoke to his family and gathered the funds together as he had been asked. Yet, when he arrived in Paris, nobody was there waiting for him. A different path was about to open in front of him, not the one he had imagined when he had answered the call. All of a sudden, he was completely abandoned in Europe at just 15 or 16, and almost penniless. His savings had ended up in the pocket of the unscrupulous agent who had taken advantage of his naivety. Sunny was alone in Paris, with no clue whatsoever about what to do next.

His first instinct was to use his last coins to get a bus to Madrid to go and stay with some people he knew. He had some old friends there, who put him up so that he could make a living doing little jobs until he got a second chance to have a go at football – which he richly deserved. That second chance came in the most unexpected way.

Sunny assembled a group of friends to represent Nigeria at the Mundialito de la Inmigración (the Immigration Mini World Cup). This popular event in the Spanish capital reflects the city's cosmopolitan nature. Agents who were looking out for raw talent would attend games and one of them was understandably impressed by Sunny. Who wouldn't have been? Luckily, there would be no deception, and no disappointment on this occasion. The agent had contacts at an Andalusian club playing in the Second Division, called Poli Ejido, in the province of Almeria. They offered Sunny a trial, which was successful, and he stayed. It took him very little time to graduate from the reserve team to senior squad, then to the starting line-up. Everything started to click for him from then on. He had the physique, he also had the personality. His outstanding progress didn't go unnoticed by the Spanish Football Federation.

He acquired Spanish citizenship, which is how he ended up playing with us at the Under-20 World Cup. He produced such sublime performances for the national team and Poli Ejido that Amedeo Carboni, the Valencia director of football at the time, who had been scouting him for a long time, offered him a long-term contract. He finally got the big break that he had been hoping and working for since leaving Nigeria.

Neither of us will ever forget the day when we joined Los Ché and were presented to the media, but it was certainly much more meaningful in Sunny's case. "I can't quite believe what I'm signing, Juan," he kept telling me. "You can't imagine what you could do with this much money in my country."

You could see in his eyes just how emotional he was in what was a once-in-a-lifetime moment, although it was tinged with sadness because his nearest and dearest were not present. I went to the Valencia office with my parents, but he was just with the agent who had discovered him in Madrid. Rather than feel sorry for himself, he uttered some moving words to me: "I'm very happy for you because your mother is here by your side, watching you sign your first contract as a professional in the top flight. It must be a tremendously proud moment for your family." He wasn't quite so lucky. I remember him calling his mother and I could hear how much she was crying at the other end of the line at home in Nigeria. She was happy because her son had finally fulfilled a dream, but also disconsolate about not being able to be there for the most important moment of his career.

It was an emotional day, not just because of what happened to me, but because I saw the life journey that Sunny had been on years after leaving Nigeria in turbulent circumstances. He had paid a hefty price to overcome the obstacles that led him to his dream. That was in stark contrast to my much more 'straightforward' path. Yes, I had to leave home when I was 15 and sacrifice some things during my adolescence, but nothing compared to what Sunny went through.

When people talk about the price to pay for being an elite-level footballer, many think that players have no reason to complain. It's a valid thought, compared with many other examples in society, but a case as tough as Sunny's shows that the jump to reach the elite can be preceded by a tricky path that may not always have a happy ending.

Everyone has a different personal experience. I wasn't subjected to a swift change of continent, from America or Africa to Europe, nor did I experience that feeling of being a complete stranger after a big shift between societies, cultures or habits. Sunny did.

From El Triunfo to Old Trafford

"Guys, don't leave after lunch, because I have something to tell you". Louis van Gaal was about to announce the arrival of a new team-mate. Some minutes later, standing in front of us, as he did every time we had lunch at the training ground, he said: "He is Marcos Rojo, a left-back who can also play centre-back, someone who is playing in the World Cup with Argentina, so please welcome him and make him feel comfortable from the first moment."

Marquitos arrived a few days later, radiating joy and happiness. He, too, had a fantastic story to tell. He comes from El Triunfo, a humble neighbourhood in La Plata, Argentina; and he's very proud of it. He used to live in a small shack made of metal panes, with all of his family.

His first memories are of playing football with whatever he and his friends could find. He and his father would cycle 10 kilometres each way to attend training – on the same bike. It was the only mode of transport available to them.

It is only when he started to impress with his local club, Estudiantes, that he got a glimpse of the escape route that would bring him out from an under-privileged background all the way to Manchester via Russia and Portugal, with Spartak Moscow and Sporting in between.

It is, again, fantastic to see how a kid full of talent but, most importantly, willpower can change his life and the life of many around him thanks to football. It doesn't matter who you are or where you come from. If you're good and have luck on your side at key moments, you can play for the best teams in the world. Which other profession, what other sport can boast of that? Sunny and Marcos arrived at the same destination as me, albeit via a different path. On top of the difficulties they encountered on the way, they had to overcome some obstacles which will be familiar to all elite athletes, whatever their background.

Dedication and the invisible

One thing unites all of us professional footballers: the knowledge that we must show real consistency to reach the top level. There are many stories involving boys who had so much potential but didn't make it because they wasted their opportunities.

Reaching the elite level involves making sacrifices and taking responsibility in a way that people outside the sport commonly forget or cannot be aware of. There are those who think: "Well, he's a footballer. It's just kicking a ball about." Well, yes, because that is what we do; and no.

As I said before, during your teenage years you have to sacrifice certain things so that you don't get left behind. That goes for football and also goes for other sports, such as gymnastics and swimming, which, on top of that, require the extra effort of a strict routine at a high-performance centre, making for an even tougher schedule than your average footballer's.

Take a gymnast who wakes up at 6am and works throughout the day. Or the tennis player who lives at a residence and does fitness training in the morning, followed by gym work and later racket work. The hours in the day are measured out according to an unforgiving plan in a bid to achieve the desired consistency in performance, as close to perfection as can be. When you're a professional sportsman you have to live with the demands linked to an unnatural level of dedication.

Of course you have to look after your own body in life and in football, but as a sportsman it's a decisive factor, one which is unique. You have to be meticulous when it comes to putting the brakes on in terms of relaxing and resting, looking after yourself, having a healthy diet and doing your gym work as necessary.

Everything revolves around your wellbeing.

If you do indulge yourself with the typical teenage activities – such as going out with friends, drinking and not getting much sleep, or no sleep at all – you may be able to cope while you're young and you may think you're physically a cut above the rest, but the human body has its own unforgiving logic, and once it levels off as an adult, all the damage done in previous years comes to the fore with devastating consequences. If you haven't looked after yourself, you won't be able to play at the level expected and your limitations will end up being clearly discernible.

On the other hand, decent fitness doesn't work if you are not mentally strong enough to cope with the demands and criticism, which will happen wherever you go. Only a fine balance between body and mind will stand you in good stead to be a professional who is able to enjoy the sport, whatever its flaws.

Inverting the week

When I moved to Madrid, it was inevitable that my new circumstances caused me to lose touch with Oviedo. Whenever I came back, I didn't really know where to go for a drink or which were the trendy places, so my friends also had to play the role of 'tour guides' in my own city, which I was forced to re-discover – especially around Oviedo's youth scene.

Later on, every year in mid-September, the phone would ring and a friend would say: "Juan, it's the San Mateo festival this weekend! (This festival, which takes place every year in the third week of September in Oviedo, includes concerts, public performances and a famous parade which commemorates the passage of thousands of Asturians to the Americas in the 19th century, and where all my friends normally reunite).

"Are you coming?"

My answer would be, sadly, pretty obvious: "Sorry guys, I can't, I have a game . . . enjoy for me."

Year after year, such phone calls from friends stopped being so regular. Any young footballer must make this kind of sacrifice in order to become a pro, but what is it compared with Sunny's odyssey to reach Valencia or Marco's road to Manchester? Not much – not much at all. Their example showed me I had no reason to complain.

It's inevitable that your youth should be far from ordinary, but, again, I wouldn't say the sacrifice was enormous in my case. What's more, it's one that can be accompanied by genuine gratification. You have to sow the seeds in order to pick the fruit later. I (we) had to rule out the very idea of a standard weekend, yes. Or, rather, my 'standard' weekend had to be different from the 'standard' for an average teenager.

From a young age, you get used to your week being inverted compared with what your peers do. It's normal to study during the week and disconnect on Saturday and Sunday. In football, all attention is focused on the weekend and that's how it's been my entire life.

Week days are for practice and preparing for the big day, the Saturday or the Sunday in the league. Showtime. That's when it counts. We have been used to it ever since we started to play football. We do love weekends too, but for different reasons. We don't have a day off then. We don't go and watch a game. We play it. And that's a great privilege which, like all privileges, comes with responsibility.

Amateurism versus professionalism

You can compare the difference between the feelings of an amateur and a professional football player with the difference between hitting a few golf balls on the practice range and putting to win at the 18th.

It is human nature that you would be able to enjoy the practice much more when the repercussions of a mistake are nothing like what happens in a game. You're just more relaxed and don't think too much. You simply enjoy yourself hitting the ball straight and making good contact. It's the same thing during childhood, when you don't feel that pressure to perform at your top level. You just want to play with your friends, just because you love it.

When you turn professional, on the other hand, those demands are paramount and condition your ability to enjoy the game. How to preserve a sense of enjoyment became key – and it still is to me. When you cross the threshold into the professional world, you are also forced into making decisions that you are not ready for and that might condition the rest of your life on and off the pitch, which is what happened when I joined Valencia at 19.

I had got through successive selection processes at Real Madrid and the experience had helped me mature swiftly, ensuring I arrived there ready for battle. And I was.

6

PASSING MY DEGREE

'Nowhere else did I learn as much about myself and others as I did on a football pitch'
– Jorge Valdano

I'm sorry to say that 19-year-old me was shaking like a leaf in my first ever press conference, on the occasion of my unveiling at Valencia. In fact, I had been pretty shocked since Sunny and I had arrived at Manises airport, straight from the Under-20 World Cup in Canada. Dozens of journalists were waiting for us and let's put it this way: we were not used to it. "Wow, it's nice to feel the expectation – but it really scares me!" I said to Sunny and his agent, or words to that effect.

We had landed back in Spain, we had also landed in the professional football media game. It didn't only mean that our responsibility on the pitch was greater. It meant interviews, press conferences – and it was just the beginning. It was all new, very exciting for sure, but 'demanding' also.

Frankly, we were completely unprepared for it. I remember that after going to the hotel, and without a lot of time to take a rest, we headed to El Corte Inglés, Valencia's biggest department store: we needed to buy some 'smart' clothes for our presentation the next day.

Fernando Valls, a fantastic person who worked (and still works) at the club in the player care department, took us to the shopping mall. After checking different options, I played safe and chose a blue jacket for the occasion, nothing flamboyant, which looking back was probably three sizes too big for me! Maybe that was the fashion back then. How could I not realise? Let's just say that it was a pretty questionable decision. And anyway, Sunny's white jacket made mine look much better. *Phew.*

After a night of little sleep, then came the ordeal of the presentation or unveiling, as you might call it. Unlike in England, in Spain new players go on to the pitch and have a few kicks of the ball in front of the supporters and photographers on the day. I didn't especially enjoy that. Nowadays, every fan expects the new player to do all kinds of skills, but, hey, there is a risk that the show can end up in a completely different way, a risk which is multiplied by ten because of the context. We've seen it many times, haven't we?

There is always a player that pretends to do something really cool, but makes a fool of himself and spills the ball after three tricky keep-ups because of the nerves and the excitement. Then the exaggerated logic of today's world starts. Somebody creates a gif, puts it online, and the 'funny' presentation will always follow that player, no matter how good he ends up being.

Sunny and I knew that so, again, we played the safe option. A few headers between us, a few runs with the ball, a few touches. 'Muchas gracias', end of story. We certainly couldn't have passed for freestylers, but we did okay under the circumstances. We were determined to show our abilities on the pitch, yes, but in the games, where it mattered.

Another example of today's 'crazy' logic is when a player kisses the badge at their unveiling, and they are automatically adored by fans. Why? Don't ask me. I don't understand it. The love for a club, from my point of view, is shown by professionalism and by giving everything you have in training and games. By respecting the values of the club. By representing the club in the best possible way. By showing commitment. Not only by kissing the badge on the very first day. Forgive me if you don't agree, but that's the way I see it. Maybe I'm wrong.

Coming back to 'our day', we posed with the new Valencia kit for the photographers and headed back to Mestalla's dressing room, after thanking all the fans that attended. We had to get ready for the media presentation.

The most 'difficult' part was yet to come: the press conference. It's natural that everyone, for the first time, is afraid to speak in public, right? I was.

My parents knew it, so they tried to relax me and told me what questions to expect, but I hadn't prepared a speech or anything. Should I have prepared something? There was no time for preparing anymore, though. It was like throwing myself in a cold swimming pool without taking a shower beforehand. At that time, I didn't like to stand up and speak in public while at school, or in front of all my team-mates, so you can imagine how I felt about what was about to start.

Cameras, journalists, speech, questions . . .

You're saved from that in England where (I believe) it isn't compulsory to organise a press conference to welcome a new player, although that did happen to me both at Chelsea and Manchester United. But despite the greater impact of those transfers in the media, it was nothing as frightening as what happened when I joined Valencia. I had more experience, for starters. Presentations, anyway, are a big thing not just because of the journalists, but also the presence of club directors and family members.

Sunny and I walked from the dressing room to the first floor of the stadium. We were unveiled in the VIP area at Mestalla. I remember the situation very well. We were seated in the front row with president Juan Soler and I had my family members just behind. They had advised me to be myself and, above all, not forget to say 'gracias'.

The president was the first to speak: "It's an honour to present to you these two young players, who are an investment in our present and future . . ." After the short introduction, we got up and we had the classic photo taken where you hold the kit.

I was in a cold sweat. It was the first time I'd had so many cameras on me. I think I could see between 20 and 30, flashing repeatedly. It was intimidating.

Don't forget, though, I was looking 'really good' and my jacket was three sizes too big. Not a great start.

That was my baptism, perhaps not quite of fire, but of something which felt very much like it at the time. I'd discovered the huge level of media interest in a club like Valencia, one of those clubs of which so much is expected, and which, consequently, is subjected to high demands and constant examination by journalists. What's more, our presentation took place during a quiet summer, with no big tournaments taking place. Given the lack of activity at the training complex, it was inevitable that our signing would become a big story.

Enduring that barrage of questions was the first challenge in my dealings with the press. Luckily, my voice didn't shake too much and as far as I can remember my answers were reasonable: there were no monosyllabic answers, though they were not very long or complicated either.

I had given a few interviews at the Oviedo and Real Madrid academies, but I had never addressed a room while standing up with a microphone in my hand, with a crowd of people observing me. I remember the situation all too clearly, but what I actually said then is now buried in an inaccessible part of my brain. That's probably a good thing.

At least there was the odd funny question that allowed us to relax for a few moments: "Given your age, does pre-season feel like a university entrance exam?" That press conference surely did.

Luckily Sunny and I both managed to pass. My parents still claim today that I did so with flying colours, as all parents would. When it was all over and I got to the hotel, I remember I was shattered from all the built-up tension and crashed down on the bed.

It wasn't a standard experience for a 19-year-old. My friends were saying to me: "If that had been me, I wouldn't have got a word out." Sunny and I got through that ordeal, but it made me realise that footballers aren't prepared well enough for such situations.

You are coached to play and perform, yes, but not to handle the obligations which go with being a top-level professional. Media being one of them. Over time I gradually took to the idea. I started playing that 'other game', giving interviews, appearing in more press conferences and, little by little, overcoming the natural fear of speaking in public. I found it easier to answer questions and elaborate my points in a calmer way. I learnt to be more myself while speaking in public. As is the case with everything, practice made me feel more comfortable in these situations.

I certainly now know the ropes when it comes to media appearances. But I had to learn along the way. I wasn't taught.

That 'other game'

Some players never enjoyed that other game. They loathe the media and hardly ever give interviews. They really dislike it.

Of course, it is a choice and I understand and agree if that's the way you are. Others don't mind interviews and have no problems giving the odd statement and making media appearances.

Then, there are those who like all that too much and are in the papers every day. They love it. It obviously takes all kinds to make a team and, in the end, it all depends on your personality. You should do what you feel comfortable with.

That being said, there are certain rules and demands, including speaking to the press from time to time, that whether you like it or not, you have to follow. The ideal scenario, should there be one, would be a middle ground where you don't do too much or too little and feel comfortable performing a task that has become an important part of our profession.

On a personal level, I've grown to try and maintain that middle ground and to be able to even enjoy the odd exercise, especially when I have a conversation with the journalist rather than a question-answer typical interview. Get me talking about football, tactics, training, routines, games, tournaments, memories, and I'll go on and on . . . I'll ask my own questions, too. I love to speak about football. As with everything, practice helps, but are footballers prepared for this from the beginning? I don't think so.

Academies don't necessary help you deal with the challenges that the media world brings. Or at least they didn't when I was learning my trade, which isn't that long ago (or it actually might be, but I don't want to accept it).

I think that more groundwork needs to be done at an earlier stage. Youngsters who are about to take the jump to a big club should be given talks about the importance of how to express themselves in the press. Something along the lines of: "It's in your hands. Be honest. Be yourself. But also be aware of possible misunderstandings.

One of these misunderstandings can lead to a bad headline, the bad headline can lead to a pretty difficult moment for the club and yourself. We all have made and we all are going to make mistakes, just be aware of it." It's about being ready for them.

As I say, nobody's born knowing everything; and to be ready could mean, for example, taking classes in public speaking.

I feel there's room for improvement in this area in youth football. Also, a foreign player who signs for the academy or even for the first-team squad would find it extremely useful to have someone help him – or her – to understand just what it means to be part of the club (to learn and understand the club's culture) and the potential exposure of his/her private life in the future. You don't just need media training, but also what I would call 'awareness training' in terms of what playing for each team entails. I find that incredibly important as I lived through it myself, as I told you at the beginning of the book.

Once you get to the first team, of course, it's a different story as every club has their media department staff. At Manchester United, as you would expect, we have many people, but mainly Karen Shotbolt and John Allen. They are with us every day in training and at games and always keep an eye on us, trying to 'protect' and advise us. At a club of this calibre, you always have to be ready to deal with the media. They help us with any issue we may have. Let's just say that they are very busy people.

Difficult beginnings

As part of this 'Masters degree' and after moving from Madrid, having enjoyed a good pre-season in Ermelo, a small town in the Netherlands where Valencia CF always used to go for a training camp, I had to wait until September 2, 2007, to play my first competitive game for my new club.

It was in Almeria that I made my La Liga debut, aged 19. I have mixed memories of that day. Good for obvious reasons (having made it to Primera División), but bad ones because it cannot have been one of my better games as I didn't play again (save for less than 15 minutes against my previous club Real Madrid, the irony of it!) until we changed managers, a little under two months later, after losing 3-0 at Sevilla and being beaten by Chelsea and Rosenborg in two Champions League games on the trot.

I had been on the bench a few times but was not even part of the matchday squad more often than not. Those were difficult moments. I, and members of my family, went so far as to question if I had made the right decision coming to the club. There was even talk of a possible loan deal to a lower-ranked side, like Getafe or Zaragoza, but I was determined to stay. Gut feeling again. There was no way I was going to leave at that time.

Quique Sanchez Flores had been the manager but the team was going through a sticky patch – as was I. It wasn't an easy season at all in terms of results and consistency of our performances, and we all know what happens normally when any club experiences a bad run of results: the situation becomes unsustainable and the coach ends up being the weakest, most expendable link.

There are numerous factors that can affect the team's performances, results being surely one of the biggest as they affect the confidence levels and the team's momentum. Also, a consistent drop in the level of performance could be caused by a negative atmosphere within the team or in the club, a lack of leadership, a certain lack of motivation, some physical issues . . . or most commonly, a mix of them all.

One brings the others and so on. You can be overcome by a sense of helplessness that prevents you from playing your normal game. You definitely want to perform well, but you feel inhibited. You know the words to the song, but no sound comes out of your mouth. Again, confidence is at the heart of it, that key word for every footballer. And, of course, given that situation, there is also sometimes that exaggerated need of pursuing who is to blame for it, who are the guilty ones . . .

Unsurprisingly, some people always end up announcing that they've found the reason: the team is not fit.

Fitness coaches are usually scapegoats. The players look tired, they seem to arrive one second late to every challenge, they don't feel as quick as they used to . . .

All of this is probably right, but the reason behind it is probably not the physical condition of the team (many fitness coaches would agree with me), but instead the mental condition of the team.

What's in charge of your body? The mind.

What can change your mind? A victory.

So, to end, we come back to the beginning: results. A winning team never feels tired.

And that's what happened at the start of my first season at Valencia. Results were not really coming for us and Quique was fired at the end of October. Ronald Koeman, who had won the title in Holland with PSV the previous season, was the man chosen to replace him.

On a personal level, I was convinced that the situation was going to turn around.

Based on how I felt in training, I really believed in myself. There were some tough days, for sure, but I was only 19. I didn't feel particularly pressed for time. I decided to wait for my opportunity – and it paid off.

Sometimes we all just need that little push

The opportunity arrived when someone told me: "Play your own game. It's got you this far already." This someone was our new manager. You always need the trust of a manager, especially in the beginning when he/she gives you your chance. We all need that little (big) push. For me, that person was Ronald Koeman. To start with, I became a regular in the matchday squad. From December onwards, I was given game time in every single league match and by the end of February, I was part of the starting XI in every game bar one, be it in the league or the Copa del Rey.

There were some big names in the Valencia dressing room who were ahead of me in the pecking order in my position, such as the great Vicente or Gavilán; but Koeman and his coaching staff, which included José Mari Bakero, one of his former Barcelona team-mates and a Spanish champion with Real Sociedad, made the brave decision to give me a chance. Looking back, this was the turning point in my career. It certainly left a mark that never disappeared.

"Don't worry, I believe in you," Koeman told me. "It doesn't matter that other members of the squad are more experienced. Status is not important for me. Enjoy yourself on the pitch, do what you know, and your confidence will grow."

His words were a real help, the kind of words which can make a huge difference for a young player.

Koeman's own experience as a footballer, I'm sure, helped him give me the right advice when he realised that I was ready, having watched me at the training ground.

"Do what you do in training. Try to play just like you train," he insisted.

This might come as a surprise for many in Valencia, where Koeman isn't fondly remembered, but I must give credit where it's due. There were some issues between him and some of the bigger figures in the dressing room, such as Albelda, Angulo and Cañizares, so the atmosphere was not ideal and the season had more downs than ups. But from a personal point of view, as I cannot speak for others, I am really grateful to him.

We ended it on a high, winning the Copa del Rey. Prior to winning this trophy in 2019, this was the last major honour Valencia had won (we beat Getafe 3-1, a game in which I had the huge pleasure of scoring the opening goal – I had also scored twice at Mestalla when we eliminated Barcelona in the semi-final in what was my first 'big night').

Koeman was sacked a little after, when we lost badly against Athletic Bilbao the following weekend. And we had not one more, but two different managers during the latter part of that season, making it four in total.

Oscar Fernandez (who was manager of Valencia's reserve team) took charge for a couple of games and then Voro (it wouldn't be his last time taking charge), the man for everything at the club, ended the season being the manager, with the pressure of saving the team from relegation with four games to go.

That's how bad it was.

As you can imagine by now, I learned many, many things (on and off the pitch) over the course of that year (in which we also had different chairmen at the club), which is why I always call it my 'Masters degree' of professional football: the Real Madrid academy scholar graduated in Valencia.

GUESS WHO?
A picture from
my early years.
A questionable
outfit, I know,
but you can
still tell it's me,
can't you?

SMILING:
I was lucky,
I had a very
happy childhood

TAKE IT AS READ:
(Left) Trying to copy my grandad, as always! (Below) with my mum and sister at my first international tournament in Tarbes, France

CLOSE:
My sister, Paula, and I have always been close. Again, I know - nice outfit, right?

FIRST STEPS: Enjoying the sunshine and fresh air – and already with a ball at my feet

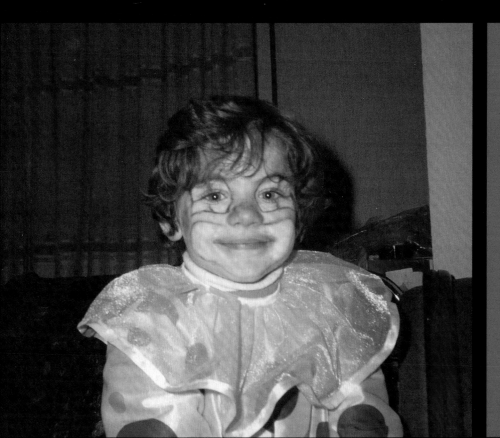

HAPPY DAYS: Playing the game for sheer enjoyment. Football should not be only about winning or losing, especially at an early age. Can you spot me?

BLUES BROTHERS: With my team-mates from the Asturian Regional Team at the National Championships

DEDICATION: I would practise for hours against a wall to improve my skills. I'd never get tired of playing football, just like now

MAGIC MEMORIES: There was always a camera on hand to capture those special moments throughout my childhood

"OPERACION ARBOL"

SCHOOL DAYS:
Celebrating victory in a local radio programme (above) – my first triumph would not come through football! (Right and below): Here I am circled with my classmates

COLEGIO LA GESTA I
OVIEDO

cajAstur

LA FABRICA: Joining Real Madrid's famous youth academy at the age of 15 helped shape my ambitions as a footballer

It wasn't easy at all, but it provided me with so many unexpected experiences that would surely help me in the future to play for the clubs that I have played for and to have the career that I've had so far.

I know that it couldn't have happened if Koeman hadn't shown confidence in me at the very beginning of my professional life.

We all need someone who believes in us.

7

UNSUNG
HEROES

'Before you can coach others, first you must learn to coach yourself' – Johan Cruyff Institute

Everything that I am as a player is a result of a learning process, along with the help and advice of some people that have been very, very important in my career. In all players' careers, there are some managers that, although not necessarily famous, played a crucial role in our development, not only as players but also as people. And it is about these coaches, and the player they helped create, that I want to talk now.

My father often tells me how he and his team-mates would go for long runs in the mountains at their pre-season training camps, without a football pitch in sight. Luckily, things have changed. For as long as I can remember, my training sessions have been geared towards rehearsing possible situations that could arise in the game, run by coaches who favour drills with the ball and wanted us to understand why we were working in that way. That's been the case ever since I was an amateur, the basis of my apprenticeship and of my development as a player. It's served me and my teams well, I think.

The element of fun was present from the beginning, as it should be, with Iñaki Artabe at La Fresneda. I also had superb coaches at the Real Oviedo academy, like Blas García, who used to call me 'pistolero' for my ability to shoot quick with my left foot, like if it was a gun; and Tomás, who would play for the B team of Atlético de Madrid as well as Oviedo, Valencia and Racing Santander as a midfielder, a player who had a remarkable gift for distribution. I started to enjoy myself under him, doing rondos in training and practising switching the play in certain pre-determined situations.

I also learnt a lot from Carlos Pérez Salvachua, Tristán Celador, Alejandro Menéndez and Michel at the Real Madrid academy. These are the people who taught me key footballing concepts which are still with me today, such as how to get over the ball before shooting. "Get under it and it'll go over, get over it and . . . goal!" the Real Madrid Under-19 C team coach Tristán used to bellow at us.

It was a simple, but efficient, command to transmit the importance of our body position when going for goal.

'Smelling' the ball

I learned, too, the importance of pouncing on loose balls if a team-mate took a shot and it rebounded. My dad used to tell me, "just like Raúl!" (Raúl Gonzalez Blanco), because he was a real opportunist who scored countless goals that way.

This is a gift that you have to work on; intuition comes with hard work. People say that Frank Lampard was the perfect example of it, always in the right place at the right moment, the man who scored so many goals by 'sniffing out' rebounds in the box. The ball would always fall to him exactly where he was. Well, few people worked harder at it than Frank. Thomas Müller has also developed that poacher's instinct. Delle Alli, too. They have a sixth sense in the box.

It isn't only a matter of luck, of course. The balls don't just drop there by chance; you have to learn to be in the right place at the right time. The ability that some players have to gobble up loose balls comes from their youth days and the coach at that time is a key part to it; my father is adamant about this (and dear father, I think you are right on this occasion).

There were many areas of my game that had to be polished over time. Academy coaching wasn't focused on 'me, me, me,' but instead the group and collective good. It was drummed into me from the beginning, at La Fresneda, Juventud Estadio, Oviedo and Real Madrid, which helped me become the player I am today. I certainly won't ever forget that, as I won't forget people like Carlos Pérez Salvachua, a young coach who liked involving the ball in training and possession-based drills. He went on to work at Villarreal and Valladolid.

Then there was our coach with the Under-19s, Alejandro Menéndez, a fellow Asturian who had made a name for himself at Sporting de Gijón. He gave me huge confidence when I was a year or two younger than the other players. It is with him that I found what it meant to compete in the División de Honor (Division of Honour), the intermediary level between amateur and professional football in Spain. Going through it really toughens you up, as you face youth and reserve players from the top teams in Spain, like Barcelona, Atleti, Valencia, Oviedo, Sporting and Sevilla . . . And when we won the 2006 Copa de Campeones (Champions Cup), which is the mini-tournament which closes the División de Honor season, it felt like winning the Champions League. It was also a very special day for me on a personal basis as I scored the winner (with a free-kick) in our 1-0 victory over Real Valladolid.

Without all of them, I would not have made it. Well, poor coaching is one of the reasons why many prospective players don't reach their target of turning professional. They may train in fantastic facilities, have the 'ideal' environment in many ways, have the physical and technical gifts you need as a footballer, but they still won't make it if they aren't taught how to think on and with their feet and develop their decision-making ability on the pitch.

Different philosophies

The youth set-ups at Ajax and Barcelona, to give two examples, are well-known examples of just that. You can see that the players have a defined style of play, based on a positional game, that they've picked up over the years and all adhere to the same philosophy. The coaching is entirely geared towards making sure that the graduates put their acquired knowledge into practice with the first team. Their philosophies of football are clear, non negotiable and forged over time.

At Real Madrid's La Fábrica, the non negotiable philosophy was also there, but not specified in one style of play, rather one specific mantra: *never ever give up*. Compete until the end. Competitiveness is something that you breathe at Real Madrid. And the first team shows that year after year.

Whether one approach is better than the other or not, I'm not able to judge myself. More to the point, I'm not convinced it is necessary to make that judgement either, as what matters the most is that their academies are able to produce a high number of players who reach the top level in their own first teams or in other clubs. I am one of these players. What it will help you do the most, for sure – and it helped me – is to adapt yourself wherever you play.

Versatile, good or bad?

Being versatile, though, can be a double-edged quality, as I've found out throughout my career. It makes your game more complete, yes. Playing in different positions also means you're probably able to understand football better, especially in terms of pattern and movement. That's good. Maybe you play more because your manager can play you in more positions. That's excellent. But on the other hand, you have the risk of not making a place your own, of not being called a specialist. That can become a problem.

Some qualities I do have, and others that I don't, make me more suitable for certain roles. It used to be that if you were right-footed, as a winger you play on the right, you cross. Not any more – this is the era of inverted wingers.

The number 10 role is where I normally felt most comfortable during my career, but I also had to adapt many times to playing on the wing. Whether I'm on the left, right or down the middle, my game involves seeking out space between the lines and trying to make the team play. I'm obviously not an old-fashioned winger (although at the beginning of my career at Valencia that's what I was) who hogs the touchline and looks for one-v-one situations . . .

I started playing down the left at Oviedo and was a striker for many years at Real Madrid academy alongside Bueno. I regularly featured for Valencia on the left wing and have played down the right most of the times I played for Spain, although I vividly remember that I made my debut down the left flank against Turkey at the Bernabeu.

Later on, I played on the left at Chelsea under André Villas-Boas, just as I had done at Valencia, but settled into the number 10 position in my second season with the Blues, after the arrival of Eden Hazard and Oscar.

Roberto Di Matteo set us up as an attacking trio, with the two of them on the wing and me at number 10. One of the first games playing like this was a 2-1 away victory at the Emirates in September 2012. I scored that day, and we had the three *enganches* on the pitch, as the South Americans say, three 'hooks', three creators.

It enabled us to have a lot of the ball and we used it well. Some people were saying before the game that 'they can't play together', especially against a big team . . . but why should it have been the case? Many had also said that Xavi and Iniesta couldn't play together. How much we would have missed out on if that was the case! Of course they could play together. Good football players always find a way to play together.

I had previously played in the hole occasionally, but it is only at Chelsea that I made it my own, initially with Roberto Di Matteo and then with Rafa Benítez, who did everything he could to give me the confidence needed to fulfill that role.

I very much enjoyed it. I loved it. And I ended up with the best figures of my career that season, with 20 goals and 35 assists. So, that's my ideal position then? Yes . . . and no.

I've also had games in which I've felt completely at ease down the right, coming inside. One example: When we beat Liverpool 2-1 at Anfield in 2015 and I scored a double. I also had some great afternoons playing down the left at Valencia and Chelsea.

What's the conclusion, then?

Yes, position does matter, a lot, as it can allow you to flourish. But I consider more important the style of play and the style of your team-mates than the actual position itself. I remember how, ahead of that game at Anfield, there was plenty of debate about whether I should play out wide or not. I did and it worked a treat. It's all relative. What matters is playing well and being surrounded by team-mates who you link up well with. It is true that my position evolved from a classic winger into a playmaker as I matured as a player.

When you play in the hole, apart from connecting the team and trying to chip in with goals and assists, one cannot forget the defensive responsibilities, particularly in terms of keeping close to the opposition's holding midfielder. For me, a number 10 should also be able to play facing his own goal and have the capacity to lay off the ball, turn and keep up the run to receive the ball again. Just like strikers do. It is a difficult position because it requires a lot, with and without the ball, but it really is a key position for any team in my view.

Some perceive the role of a number 10 as being more about your head than your feet, but I would say that applies to football as a whole. For me, in any case, it's always been about the flow of the game, which might not always be spectacular. But many of football's most important aspects are not spectacular or exuberant. It's not all about speed (physical), like some want us to believe.

For example, slowing the game down also gives you a chance to accelerate at the right moment, create an imbalance that wasn't obvious to the eye to start with, that perhaps wasn't even there. A tempo change can be a game-changer. To stop is as important as to accelerate. The speed that matters the most is the mental speed.

Studying football

There are footballing principles which are valid in all coaching contexts. One which sticks out for me is that it's important for players to understand and try to switch the ball from side to side, play in such a way that disrupts the opponents' shape and execute a penetrating pass that will create space – the one thing footballers feed on more than any other.

It works only based on logic. If one side of the pitch is 'busy' with players, the other side will be emptier, and so it would be better to try to attack through there. As nobody can move as quick as the ball does, the principle of playing quick and switching the ball to the other side seems like a pretty obvious and clear tactic. It is not so easy to execute, though. Playing quick is not quite the same as playing quick and precise, which is what is required to be most effective on a football pitch. Hence, it's harder to do.

'Collective skills', to me, as I've said before, matter as much as individual talent, even if individual talent must be nurtured and cherished and can be the decisive factor. But there's too much attention given to it today and, as a consequence, learning as a united group isn't given as much importance as it deserves. It's a mistake to neglect the fact that you need 11 players to form a football team, to forget that our sport doesn't solely revolve around individual brilliance, even if individual brilliance can unlock a situation.

If coaches fail to transmit that message, it only serves to feed the players' egos. If you're always and constantly told that you're a great finisher, and all you should do is shooting, you'll end up shooting all the time when the best option may be to pass to a team-mate. Understanding how to use the ball matters more than anything else; it is an internal decision-making process that has to be refined throughout your career, particularly in the early stages.

A player should ideally develop his/her knowledge and understanding of the game at the same time as his/her physical, technical and tactical attributes, as it will probably be too late to do so when he or she reaches the professional stage. It follows that gaining a deep understanding of the game during that developmental stage is such a huge asset compared to having to learn when you're, in theory at least, already the finished product.

It's never too early for that. Youngsters are perfectly capable of assimilating those concepts. If a child is told, "when you receive the ball here, try to release it into this area", "if you don't have a pass option, wait until the opponent comes and then divide the play", "give a pass line to your team-mate", "understand the moments of the game, play with the tempo", then he/she will gain a fast understanding of what he/she needs to do for the team's benefit.

Game intelligence

Of course, at eight, 10, 12 or 15, you are yet to develop the mental maturity required to become a well-rounded footballer: you are acquiring your future shape, so to speak, which is why, at that stage, the mind plays a key role in defining your game and enabling you to take on a range of responsibilities on the pitch.

I've seen academies where the focus was on making the most of each player's individual attributes, but not enough effort was put into ensuring that their best talents had a real grasp of the game. It won't help those players later in their careers, when game intelligence becomes a determining factor.

At those ages, you may make mistakes that you can compensate for with your technical ability. That's great. But that's also a problem, because if you then believe that this will help you in the rest of your career, you're making a big mistake. What looks like ability may, in fact, be a defect that will have a negative bearing on your long-term future. The key is to keep learning constantly.

When a footballer feels superior to the rest – and I include myself in that group as I, too, have made that mistake in the past (when winning with good teams against lower teams was 'easy') – he/she may try to do more than he/she should on the pitch, what is usually called 'showboating'.

This is a sure way to commit errors that can harm the team, and could also harm the player's reputation and career.

There will be some who think that the player who has the most tricks in his locker is the star, but for me that's not always the reality. What's the point of doing three stepovers to mock your opponent if it is to play a one-yard sideways pass afterwards?

Throughout my career, apart from those I've already mentioned, I've also had coaches who have drummed the importance of understanding the game into me. Luis Milla, Indonesia's national team head coach at the time of writing, and Sevilla's manager Julen Lopetegui, for example, did it in the national youth teams and the senior national team. It is a fact that Spain's system has been geared towards the tactical education of players for a long time.

The method

If you're looking for the key to the beautiful football and the unprecedented success enjoyed by *La Roja* from 2008 onwards, look no further. It is the footballing education that we all received coming up through the youth ranks at international level, thanks to people like them and the youth team co-ordinators like Ginés Meléndez.

When I was a teenager, I absolutely loved getting called up. All you wanted was to do well in your team so you would maybe have the chance of being called up by your country.

My first time, when I was 15 and playing for Real Oviedo's academy, we went to a tournament in the Canary Islands. Right from the start, we always felt that we were one of the favourites to win every competition we competed in. Everyone respected the Spanish team, something that never quite happened at the senior levels at the time. It was difficult to explain because people wondered how we could be so successful at youth level and yet never able to translate that superiority further down the line.

Thankfully, time would end up being the best possible answer for that.

Spain has an impressive collection of Under-17, Under-19 and Under-21 Euro titles, and that is not by coincidence. There is the talent, of course, there is also good camaraderie (bear in mind that you basically made new friends every time you were called up), but there is also the work of the coaches, the methodology, the model of play and the competitive gene that is now part of Spanish football's DNA.

Most of the coaches always made me feel at home while with the national team and showed great faith in me, so much so that they moved me up to play in older age groups very often, which would help me to develop as a player. I played the Euros at Under-19 and the World Cup at Under-20 with the generation one year older than me, and I featured with the Under-21s as an 18-year-old, for example.

I felt important growing up in the Spanish model of football, and that helped me a lot to believe in my capacities and to grow year after year. I remember how, especially in the earlier years, when I was 15 and 16 years old, we would have 'trial' games in Madrid on the Monday and Tuesday every three months, in which we would be selected or not for the official tournament. I was nervous, of course, I wanted to impress them, but there was also so much talent around.

As you can imagine, that meant you would be missing school times (I would travel to Madrid on Monday and would be back to Oviedo on Wednesday), so as I told you earlier on, Ginés personally gave us lessons (he was also a teacher) in maths, geography, whatever was needed to balance out our education.

Off the pitch, he would also speak about how important the character, the will and the determination would be for us to make it into professional players. On the pitch, he and the other coaches would encourage us to express ourselves, to take good care of the ball, to pass and move, to search for and give pass lines, to think quick and make good decisions with and without the ball, to react quick and press the opponent when losing the ball . . . in other words, they were 'teaching us' the Spanish model step by step.

Ginés, Iñaki Sáez (who would be Senior National Coach at Euro 2004 after winning many trophies with the youth teams), Milla, Fernando Hierro and Lopetegui (amongst others) would be key figures for the development of Spanish football, and needless to say, also very important for myself.

These people are some of the (not so) unsung heroes behind Spain's blossoming as a dominating force on the international stage.

8

LA ROJA

'Nobody cares for the All Blacks, the All Blacks take care of themselves' – 'Legacy: 15 Lessons In Leadership' by James Kerr

July 11, 2010. World Cup final. Minute 116: The sound of silence . . .

Everyone on the bench stands up, we feel that something special can happen. Fernando controls the ball, raises his head, and sees Andrés Iniesta making a run on the right. He tries a difficult pass . . . the ball does not find its recipient at first. Rafael Van der Vaart, their captain, intercepts it, losing his balance and leaving it, luckily, for Cesc. We are closer to their goal. Much closer . . .

After a touch, Cesc finds Andrés on the right, who is alone and inside the box. Van der Vaart reacts quickly after losing his balance, but it is already too late. Andrés' first touch is not good. The ball jumps a bit high, but in a perfect position to shoot . . . time stops . . .

Millions of people holding their breath.

I see everything in slow motion.

Please, Andrés, put it in. Please, Andrés.

Two men, one goal, one ball. That's all it is right there and then. Nothing else matters. He shoots. Not only with the power of his right foot, but with the power of hundreds and hundreds of Spanish players who paved the way, dreaming of this moment (but never living it); with the power of millions of Spanish people who want to feel proud, finally, about their national football team; with the power of our dreams.

Stekelenburg touches the ball, but cannot stop it. Not a single human could stop a shot with such emotional power. Only Andrés, ball and goal now. I look at the linesman. The flag stays down. The ball smashes the net. I run like I've never run before. We all go towards Andrés. I scream as I run, I am exploding . . .

I jump on the rising mountain of players, with Andrés (I imagine) choking out of sight at the bottom of the pile. We are all yelling, crying, shouting, sobbing . . . but around us, silence. Or should I say, Dutch fans (who were in a big majority in the stadium). I will never forget that moment, I have it stuck in my mind. I heard the sound of silence.

Campeones del Mundo: A 36 hour day

Howard Webb whistles for the end of the game. We are World Champions. Yes, 'Campeones del Mundo.' For the first time in our history, Spanish football reaches the top. Screams, tears, jumps, hugs . . . we have done it. *What, really? Have we just won the World Cup? Us?* We couldn't believe it. We just couldn't.

Not until we touched that cup. *THE* cup. Not until we lifted it to the sky. Really, not until we came back to Spain . . . The celebrations in South Africa, on the pitch, were incredible, but we were in shock, we couldn't digest it. That's why, if you ask me, the following day, the homecoming in Madrid after winning the final, was without doubt one of the most beautiful days of my life; when we realised what we had done.

The plane, the 'World Cup Winners' plane, lands in Madrid's airport on July 12, 2010, hours after the final. We look out through the windows, the place is packed. Hundreds of people waiting for us, airport workers, police, firemen . . . and the bus, our bus, the open-top bus.

The parade through the streets of the capital was simply an unbelievable experience, something which I struggle to find the right words to describe, something unrepeatable if you like, something unique. Just thinking about it now, while writing these lines, still gives me goosebumps, the euphoria, the wild joy, the exhilaration of it all.

The day began with the de rigueur formal visits to the Prime Minister and King Juan Carlos, before we headed to the centre of Madrid, through the district of Moncloa to Calle Princesa, Plaza de España, Gran Vía, until Puente del Rey. I'd passed by those streets hundreds of times in my life. Well, of course, this time was different.

There wasn't an inch of space that wasn't occupied by people on those wide avenues. Balconies were packed with people waving and cheering at us. Hundreds of thousands of people accompanied us along the way. From the top deck, it looked like a human tide. It *was* a human tide. Unforgettable.

Spain had already staged a dress rehearsal for these

celebrations after winning Euro 2008 two years earlier. I hadn't been involved in that tournament myself, I was playing for the Under-20s at that time, but my team-mates had told me that, yes, the celebrations in Madrid had been something extraordinary – but still, could not compare to the explosion of joy generated by winning the World Cup. The first World Cup. There is only one first time, after all.

Following the public celebrations, the day finished with a party for all members of staff, players, families and friends. Winning the final, lifting the cup, celebrating in the dressing room, a nine-hour flight back, the parade around Madrid, a party with our people . . . late at night, when I came back to the hotel and as I was lying in bed, with my body wanting and needing to sleep and my mind trying to settle down, I realised how a day can last more than 24 hours. Ours certainly did.

The World Cup once again showed me the huge emotional impact football has and how much of a unifying force it is, something which resonated even more in the context of what was happening away from football fields at that time.

Our win coincided with the onset of a global financial crisis which hurt Spain particularly badly and devastated our country's economy.

Some people talk of sports in general, and football in particular, as if it were a modern form of 'the opium of the people', that politicians might sporadically use to divert the focus from some other and more problematic matters, but, on the other hand, what's wrong with letting yourself ride on a wave of collective happiness? Nothing, I would say.

Our victory helped so many Spaniards forget about their problems, at least for some days – much longer than that, in fact. Is football that important, or as some have said, is it the most important thing out of the least important things?

The beginning of the dream

Of the many fond memories I have of playing with the Spanish national team, two stand out from the rest. The first is my debut at the Santiago Bernabéu in a World Cup qualifier against Turkey on March 28, 2009.

I was a 20-year-old gaining my first cap, wearing the number 6 shirt, Iniesta's number (Andrés was not available on that occasion), as it was one of the options that was given to me, so I felt excited to choose it.

It was not my first experience with the senior national team, though, as I had received my first international call-up back in November of the previous year, for a friendly against Chile played in Villarreal – but had stayed on the bench on that occasion.

How I found out that I was called up for the first time I will always remember: after training, in the dressing room at Mestalla. How much of a surprise it was for me you'll guess when I tell you that I didn't even know that the list was going to be announced that day.

I was in the shower when Voro, the great Voro, our match delegate, came over to tell me the news. "Juan, are you here? Come out one moment, you've been selected!"

Wait . . . what? "Yes, you are going with the national team." I jumped out of the shower, checked my phone and indeed, to have almost a hundred messages was not a usual thing to happen.

After speaking with my family, I was then photographed

holding a Spain kit, as is tradition for every new player that gets called up, with the images appearing all over the press.

Imagine, 20 years old and being selected for the senior team. It was a day of pure joy for me, the polar opposite of when I was sobbing in the shower and vowing to do everything possible to get back into the national team, after I had been left out of the Under-17 Euros squad.

It would be the culmination of a long journey up through the youth ranks, from Under-15 level all the way up to the A team. I was fully aware of exactly what it meant to fulfill that dream at such a young age. Earning a spot in the national team back then was exceptionally difficult, given that the country had a generation of outstanding players who had just been crowned European champions. The dream had only just started . . .

Every minute counts

The other highlight, as it could not be any other way, was my goal in the Euro 2012 final against Italy. It was a gift from my friend Fernando Torres, who laid it on a plate for me.

It had been a great month for us, obviously, but also a frustrating tournament on a personal level, as I hadn't featured in any of the previous matches and my expectations of participating were higher this time around . . .

So yes, there I was, watching the Euro final from the bench, supporting my team-mates, enjoying the match (our best game in the tournament), but deep inside really wanting to participate also. With us 2-0 up, Javi Miñano, our fitness coach, comes to me: "Juan, go to warm up." *Yes! That's my chance, I'm going to play!* 3-0 and I kept warming up. Sprints up and down the sideline, stretching . . . all I was waiting for was for the manager to look at me. *Come on Vicente, please, put me on.* I was desperate to get a taste of the action. I could barely contain myself as the minutes ticked by, but Del Bosque's body language gave little reason for optimism. He was following the game very carefully and I really thought he had forgotten I was warming up.

Then suddenly, with three or four minutes to go, he called me. I was finally sent on. Andrés Iniesta, the MVP of that final, *the magician*, was coming off. Handshake with Andrés, and there I was, making my debut in the Euros in the actual final. I wanted to touch the ball, I wanted to take advantage of every second of that history-making game.

Within seconds of coming on (and as I write I don't remember if I had touched the ball yet), Xavi plays a fantastic pass (one of those special Xavi passes) to Fernando Torres, and he is one against one with Buffon.

I looked for the pass, I am only metres behind him and I scream like I've never screamed before. *"Fernandooooooooo"* . . . He surely had to hear me. He just had the goalkeeper to beat, but he is too nice to try himself (he had already scored the third goal). So he lays the ball off to his right (he did hear me), eliminating Buffon from the play, and I find an empty goal in front of me . . . 'All' I had to do was push the ball into the empty net. I did it. 4-0, 88th minute and I run to him . . .

"It's yours Fer, I love you, thank you."

Bless him, particularly as he was going for the Golden Boot (which I'm relieved to say he won anyway). He would later tell me that he knew it was me and that if not, maybe he would have tried to score himself. I would call that a very good friend, wouldn't you? The last minutes of the game pass by, and we are champions again. I've played, I've scored, I'm in heaven. You never know what can happen on a football pitch in just a few minutes, I can tell you that by experience. Every minute does count.

Golden years

This very special goal would bring a perfect cycle of winning back-to-back Euros either side of the World Cup to an end. It's a feat no other European country has ever accomplished.

If you think about it, it's incredible. From 2008 until 2012 it was Spain, Spain and more Spain. And I was lucky enough to be part of most of it.

Yes, it was a great achievement to be part of such a strong squad, probably the best squad we ever had, and to live the best experiences you can ever live thanks to football, lifting the most important trophies there are. But it also meant that it was even more difficult to get a place in the team. In addition to that, I was 22 years old at the World Cup, 24 at the Euros . . . I was quite young.

Those are the main reasons I find to explain why the importance that I've had at my respective clubs hasn't necessarily always been reflected on the international stage in terms of appearances. Of course, I wanted to play, and I felt sometimes frustrated about not getting more game time (as any player would), but again, we were all in the same position, all very good players, and not everyone could play . . .

The privilege of being part of the 23-man squad, however, more than compensated for my occasional frustration. The attitude that we all had to chip in was the key to the team's success over that period. "Let's savour this, train hard and enjoy it both on and off the pitch. Let's take stock of what we're achieving here," was the message we kept telling one another.

I was fully committed during every training session and every minute when I was on the pitch; I understood that the lack of opportunities was obviously linked to the extraordinary level of competition for places in the starting XI – those who were playing were doing brilliantly – and I felt fortunate to be experiencing the best period in the history of our national team at first hand.

After all, I was part of a unique generation and felt genuinely honoured to be around so many top-level footballers, including many who are among Spain's greatest-ever players. Together, from 2008 until 2012, we made history, we touched the sky, we conquered the football world. Nobody can take that away from us.

Stepping back to move forward

As I recognised earlier, Spain's golden era was undoubtedly connected to the painstaking efforts that were put in for well over a decade in the youth ranks, where a culture of winning, and of winning well, took root. A model of play was installed in the culture of Spanish football.

One example of it. Summer 2011. Javi Martinez and me, already selected on a regular basis with the senior team and after being world champions, were asked by Fernando Hierro if we wanted to play with the Under-21s for the Euros in Denmark that was about to start.

Both of us took two seconds to respond: "Of course". The

memories were that good, the camaraderie was that strong, that it was a pleasure to 'go back' in time and re-unite with many friends, such as Ander Herrera and David de Gea. There haven't been many cases of players winning the World Cup and then competing with the Under-21s shortly afterwards, they told me. Thierry Henry did it with France in 1998 and that was about it, as far as I knew.

From the outside, some people may have thought, 'Look at these two, they're here to be seen and enjoy the ride, but they won't be guaranteed to win the tournament simply because they come from the A team.' Yet, we integrated ourselves quickly into the squad, just like the rest of our team-mates, and it turned out to be a fabulous experience. We played some great football, we very much enjoyed our time on and off the pitch, and ended up winning the trophy.

Of course, it was not straightforward because the press, as expected, piled on some pressure because we had two World Cup winners in our ranks, and for some we were supposed to win at a canter. But football does not work that way. I am very proud of that experience and, looking back now, it was definitely the right decision. We would not have made it if it wasn't for all the great work and experience we had in the national team youth system. If it wasn't for the method.

Olympic 'failure'

Talking about other competitions that I've played in with the youth teams at national level, I was also part of the team that went to the London Olympics in 2012, after winning the Euros in that memorable final against Italy. Again, I did it voluntarily, but considering it was such an occasion, it was the only decision that I had in my mind: I wanted to be an Olympian if I ever had the chance. And I did.

The whole experience was incredible – if it wasn't for the results in our games. We were a generation that had been champions in the Under-21 Euros the summer before – there was, understandably, a lot of expectation on our shoulders.

The highlight of our experience in London was the opening ceremony, and that says it all … Sharing the life of other athletes in the Olympic Village, at least for one day, was another great experience, but yes, the results and performances didn't meet our expectations, as we finished bottom of our group with zero victories and zero goals.

Two defeats against Japan and Honduras, and one draw in the last game with Morocco at Old Trafford, was our dis-appointing participation in the London Olympic Games 2012. Not good enough. But hey, I am an Olympian after all. Another box ticked.

Our identity

The fact that I was able to play the game during an era in which Spain have had a clear and recognised identity, and everyone knew perfectly well what our style of play was about, does not mean that it was always the case.

In the decades of the 1980s and '90s, Spain was not near the top of the football world. In fact, far from it. Our 'style' of play was not clear, our results were not good enough, our confidence was not high. There was even a general perception that our national team was not able to surpass the quarter-finals at the biggest competitions. Well, it was based on fact, so it was actually not only a perception, it was true.

Journalists and football 'experts' always mentioned courage as one of the main characteristics of our national teams. No trace of an actual style of play. Until Euro 2008, where everything changed.

Luis Aragonés was very much responsible for that. Especially for picking a squad in which talented players were in the majority, in which technical quality and understanding of the game mattered more than the physical attributes, and for creating a bond and togetherness among all the players and staff that would be key in lifting the trophy after 44 years of nothingness.

Of course, like always in football, chance played its part, but Luis had put all the right ingredients in the mix.

From a physical and courage-based approach, to possession with a purpose. From not dominating the games to being the masters of the game. From not going beyond the quarter-finals to winning.

Not everything was as easy as it seems, though. I vividly remember the critics that Luis had to suffer months prior to the tournament.

"You have the possession but you don't win." "You are a boring team." "You don't have the personality to compete at the highest level," were a common denominator among journalist sand fans. But Luis knew he was right and he fought for it.

There was also a big uproar about Raúl Gonzalez, the great Real Madrid striker who wasn't called up when many people believed he should be there. Luis also had to overcome that prickly situation.

The best example of the negative and reluctant atmosphere that was present only weeks before starting the competition was in the last friendly game before that tournament, a game against the USA at El Sardinero in Santander, which Spain won 1-0 (our 16th game on the trot without defeat, but even that wasn't enough to pacify the critics), right before the team headed to Neustift, our Austrian base camp. The team got booed off that game, and it didn't seem like the best 'good luck' message from the country to the players. Nobody expected what would happen in the coming weeks . . . No-one but Luis.

That team went on to win the tournament against the odds, with a brand of attacking football that was praised the world over.

It was an achievement that contributed to strengthening a team that had previously experienced many setbacks. It was an achievement that changed the course of history. We now had an identity.

That penalty shoot-out

To be fair, what really helped to change the mindset of the players and of a whole country during Euro 2008 was the game against Italy in the quarter-finals. Better said, the penalty shoot-out after the game. We believed that we could win after that day.

Italy held us to a 0-0 draw after extra time, so the game headed to the lottery of spot-kicks . . .

Gianluigi Buffon in goal, probably the best goalkeeper in the world at that time, it really seemed like a very difficult task. But we won. We did it. The curse was over. We were ready to take over the world.

That day, the day where everything started.

So alike and so different

Representing your country is definitely a different experience than playing with your club. But, why is it?

Obviously, when you play for a national team, the majority of the people of that country will support you. It doesn't matter if they like football or not, or if they support different clubs within the domestic competition, they will forget those rivalries for the moment and will join forces to support their national team. That is something that will happen in every single country in the world, but there are also some differences when speaking about different national teams, depending on the countries.

One is the tradition of where to play. I mean, in Spain, the national team does not have a national stadium per se, as we move around the country and play in many different stadiums. Is that good or not?

If what you look for is to bring the national team closer to the people, and to give everyone the chance to go and watch the side live, that is fantastic. Madrid, Sevilla, Valencia, Alicante, Oviedo . . . they consider it a privilege to get to watch us play in the flesh, and from the Spanish Federation they feel that every Spaniard has the right to enjoy the national team in their home city.

It is a valid argument, of course, but the negative side, if there is one, is that the national team will never feel like they play in their 'national stadium'. I personally like moving around grounds, but I can understand that this is a valid argument.

England always play at Wembley. 'Their' stadium, 'their' home. Also, it is the stadium where the FA Cup semi-finals and finals are played, as well as other showpiece games. To be honest, it is pretty special to play at such a venue.

But I suppose the downside of this is that if people want to go and watch the team play live, they will have to travel to London to watch the games, and if you live in the north of the country, that's not very convenient.

In my view, both approaches are valid and it is only a matter of tradition or preference. But what's your opinion? Which approach do you find more appropriate?

A big disappointment

Having already played at two World Cups, a Euros and two Confederations Cups, the blow of not being selected in the Euro 2016 squad was perhaps a bit less painful, though still very sad news for me.

I found out during a pre-match stay at the Lowry Hotel in Manchester. I was in David de Gea's room chilling and chatting with the 'Latin group': Marcos Rojo, Sergio Romero, Guillermo Varela, Ander Herrera and David himself. While talking, we had lost notion of time and didn't realise we had just missed the announcement, even though we were waiting for it.

Suddenly, David took a look at his mobile to check his messages and blurted out: 'The squad has been announced!' My body tensed. He started going through the names (his name was one of the first as a goalkeeper) and, all of a sudden, his face froze . . . "F***, you aren't there, bro . . ."

He fixed his eyes on the screen once again to check that he hadn't made a mistake and lifted his head.

"You're not there!"

My initial reaction was a shock. I grabbed hold of the squad list and went through it from top to bottom to no avail. It was true, I was not there, I was not going to Euro 2016. Probably, surely, what made me feel so sad about it, were the expectations I had created in my mind. I thought I would go, and somehow with some justification. I had been playing regularly for my club, I'd played every Premier League game that season, and finished with ten goals and 11 assists in all competitions. Not bad. I'd also played in our last three qualifiers for the Euros, as well as in the three friendlies which had followed, so I felt I was in a good position to go . . .

And David thought it too. He was obviously pleased to have been selected himself, but I knew he was gutted for me. We'd both imagined and wished that we'd be together in France, but it was not going to happen after all.

At that moment, I must accept that it was an enormous disappointment which, hard as I tried, I couldn't shake off for some time, but I also understand that national team coaches always have a really difficult task on their hands. In fact, I do not bear any grudge towards Vicente del Bosque for what happened, and, of course, overall I have plenty of reasons to be thankful to him, irrespective of my temporary disagreement (you know by now that we players tend to think that we are always right) over that decision.

He was the person who showed faith in me when I was only 20; he was the person who handed me my debut; he was the coach who took me to all the competitions between 2009 and 2014 and gave me the best experience a football player could wish for . . .

I respected the decision and knew that it was something out

of my control, of our control as players, so there was nothing else I could do other than digest the bad news and simply try to have a good end to the season so I could then enjoy the summer rest. Not everything had happened as I had wished, but I had to keep going.

Despite these natural frustrations along the way, it doesn't mean that I didn't want to thank him after he announced his retirement. I sent him a message through Maria José Claramunt (I didn't have his number), the national team director at the time. It was the least I could do.

'Please tell Vicente I'm very thankful for everything, for the faith he showed in me throughout this period and I wish him all the best for the future.' That's just how I felt, it was the right and honest thing to do, even more so because I consider Del Bosque such a good man. My parents always insisted in telling me: you have to be grateful in life. They were right, once again.

So close yet so far away

When you play abroad, far from your home country, as I've said many times, it becomes a great experience as a player and as a person, you learn a lot about other football and culture, you definitely grow as a player and as human being. But also, it has some other, let's call them, 'side-effects' that might not be as positive as all the above.

One example. Interestingly, revealingly even, there was more of a surprise in England than in Spain when I was left out of the Euro 2016 national team squad. As I've mentioned before talking about the 2010 World Cup, my name had been barely mentioned in the predicted teams doing the rounds in the Spanish press ahead of the tournaments where I would finally make the cut. They normally assumed that I wouldn't make the grade, something I would find quite funny later on when their predictions would not come true.

But it is a fact that I've noticed how, ever since moving to the Premier League, irrespective of the fact that the English clubs where I've played enjoyed success at both domestic and European level, I've receded from the daily scene in Spain, with the English (and international) media and fans taking me more into consideration than their Spanish counterparts.

What a paradox: increasing my profile internationally works the opposite way in my homeland. This is something which is probably to be expected, as losing some credit in Spain is an inevitable consequence of not playing in La Liga, not just for me, but for all Spaniards who choose to play football elsewhere. We fade in to the background, 'recede' in the public eye, which although understandable, still seems rather odd for some, as for example in my personal experience, I have played for genuinely big clubs, Chelsea and Manchester United, which undoubtedly have big reputations in England and all over the world.

The crude reality is that if you aren't on the weekly La Liga highlights show, if you are not constantly in front of people's eyes, many won't value you enough to be called up to the national team; and that's that.

Some Spanish players might have a magnificent season in England, or other foreign leagues, but will receive little recognition in their own country. Had they been playing in Spain, with the same kind of performances, their names would have been all over the newspapers in articles demanding their inclusion in the national team squad. We are a 'funny' country in that way.

Things have changed over the years, though, as there was a time not so long ago when around half the national team squad played in the Premier League. But if I was lucky enough to represent Spain during my time in England (which I value a lot for all the reasons explained above), other players who probably deserved to do so were not. They were 'too far away' from the domestic spotlight.

Maybe the biggest example of that was Mikel Arteta, a key player for Everton and Arsenal for many years, who played for every Spanish youth team but was never called up to play for the senior team. I am quite sure that if Mikel had the same kind of career as he had in England, in Spain, he would have been called up. This is not a criticism, it is a reality, probably a natural and logical reality (again, since when you disappear in a 'day to day' sense from a place, it seems reasonable that you lose importance there). Sometimes that might feel unfair, even disappointing, but you have to learn to deal with it.

Hope is the last to die

I still want to play for the national team, I refuse to think my time is over. I'm a realist, I know it's not easy, but I'm not over the hill yet and I keep the hope alive that my international career still has some way to go. Obviously, years go by, new generations of players arrive, but I honestly still feel excited and eager to return. Again, the decision depends on my manager, but what does depend on me is my belief, my desire, and my football, and I'm determined to keep trying to keep the flame lit, that's for granted. Time will tell . . .

9

THE NOMAD

'The world is a book, and those who do not travel read only one page' – Augustine of Hippo

'Juan, you will love London. You'll see, we know you.' These were the words my friends said to me on that pretty, empty beach of El Saler, just south of Valencia, the day before I flew to London to start a new life on English soil.

Years later, writing this, I can confirm they were pretty accurate, although they weren't able to predict that I would also later enjoy another English city, Manchester.

It certainly was a completely different journey from the car trip from Oviedo to Madrid that I took as a teenager. This time round, I didn't feel apprehensive or scared, but excited and far more confident. I was full of curiosity ahead of the new challenge, looking forward to discovering and enjoying the Premier League and to getting to know London for the first time.

I had never had the chance to visit the British capital properly before that. Yes, I'd been there twice before, in August 2007, but only when Valencia played in a pre-season tournament at the Emirates, and then in December of the same year when we faced Chelsea in a Champions League group game. I remember that my friend Sunny played that night and I'd come off the bench for a quarter of an hour in a 0-0 draw – but that was it.

My friends had been there on a classic boys' trip, one of those plans that I had to miss due to my professional commitments. As soon as they found out that London would be my next destination, they all gave me glowing reports of the city.

I remember that conversation on the beach so vividly, when we were wondering what life at Chelsea would be like for me. "What will it be like to go into the dressing room and see the likes of Drogba, Terry, Lampard and Čech?" we asked ourselves.

Until then, in no way had I imagined I would end up sharing a dressing room with these kind of players one day. I had been fortunate to have played alongside some great footballers at Valencia, like Fernando Morientes, David Villa, Joaquín, Vicente, Albelda, Baraja, Marchena, Silva, just to name a few, and many others in the national team, but this was different.

The prospect of sharing a dressing room with guys who had made such a mark on English and European football within a few years of Roman Abramovich arriving at the club still seemed very foreign to me, as if it were something exotic, kind of distinct from all that I had experienced previously. Yet, the Premier League, which had appeared on the horizon like an unattainable target, was about to become my new environment.

With just a few hours to go until my flight to London, I found myself discussing just how much I admired and respected those players, even from a distance.

On this occasion, like I said, fear was not present. Instead, what had taken over was a feeling of palpable excitement about the change of scene, and about starting a new, different chapter in my life.

On the move

Today, for an elite footballer, a nomadic lifestyle is what people call 'a given' and, in my own way, I had sampled it long before I signed my first pro contract, in the shape of the destinations that my father had taken us to when he was a footballer himself: Burgos, Salamanca, Cartagena and Orihuela.

My own progress, of course, had already seen me passing through Oviedo, Madrid and Valencia before I boarded my flight to London. As you would expect, I had to adapt to every new situation and I had experienced varying levels of difficulty along the way.

The first move was particularly tough because of the age. Swapping Madrid for Valencia was special because it represented my first taste of belonging to a professional dressing room in which players of all ages were present. It was the first time I felt what it meant to be part of the senior squad of a big team, and the personal relationships that this naturally entailed between players. It made me become more mature instantly.

Moving from Valencia to London was again different, since I was already a bit older as well as an established player at a good point in my career. I wasn't just changing clubs, but leagues, countries, cities, languages and lifestyle. That can have an effect on you on many levels, of course, but I really saw it as a genuine challenge, something to feel excited about. Later, the same went for my transfer from Chelsea to Manchester United, even if it occurred in completely different circumstances.

Each switch required a mental and personal readjustment, just like any other changes in life, but magnified by the power of football: you *have* to perform no matter what.

The 'adaptation process', although naturally needed, doesn't seem to be part of the formula, especially when expectations are high. Of course, at that moment, I was thrilled to say that I was going to play for such a huge club, something which would have seemed surreal to me just a few years earlier. Sometimes, I must confess it still does. I am living a kid's dream . . . and it is not always easy to see it as a reality.

London calling

"Wow!" The first impression London made on me can be summed up in that one word. London is many cities in one. It definitely surpassed expectations.

While I was living in a hotel trying to find my new home, (a period that lasted one month), I visited many places and realised how many different atmospheres, styles and cultures were co-existing together in this metropolis.

What a fascinating place to live, I said to myself. It was a lot of fun to experience it. To start with, the city's immense size allowed me to rediscover my anonymity. I would leave training and become just another Londoner, and I loved it. Yes, you could be stopped and asked for a photo or an autograph sometimes, but by no means as often as in Spain. That allowed me to enjoy the city at my own pace. It was easier to walk the streets alongside so many people of so many different origins without necessarily being recognised.

It's a global epicentre and you can feel it on every single street. It really is, though, a difficult city to get from one place to another at certain times, so I sometimes took the train to Waterloo and then the tube, as it was the best way to get into central London from my flat in Battersea at rush hour.

I tried to explore a new corner of the city every day, when I could: Chelsea, Pimlico, Richmond, Mayfair, Notting Hill, Primrose Hill, Hampstead, Shoreditch, Soho, Camden, Little Venice, Wimbledon, Kensington . . . I found it remarkable how I could go from one place to another and it would be completely different, just by travelling a few miles.

As one of the biggest cities in the world, London also offers an incredible variety of music and art events.

I remember going to see Coldplay and the Rolling Stones at the O2 Arena, visiting what would become one of my favourite spots in Soho, Ronnie Scott's Jazz Club, and attending the Tate Modern, the National Gallery, the Victoria and Albert Museum and the Saatchi Gallery on King's Road. You just couldn't finish it all.

I would say that I tried to embrace its unique melting pot of cultures and nationalities. As Samuel Johnson said: "When a man is tired of London, he is tired of life."

I wouldn't dare to disagree.

The Mancunian way

But a footballer's career can change in a matter of days – and that's what happened to mine. It was time to bid farewell to London, as I did in January 2014 when I moved within the country.

The destination was Manchester. Or, I should say as I soon found out, *friendly, creative, special* Manchester. The city also corresponded to an image of the English city that I had conjured up in my mind: red-brick buildings, factories, industrial revolution-style. In a way, Manchester allowed me to immerse myself more deeply in English culture than London's cosmopolitan vibe had.

There was the music, from Joy Division, The Smiths, and Stone Roses to Oasis, whose presence and legacy is palpable in so many places in the city.

'A nation's culture resides in the hearts and in the soul of its people' – Gandhi

Now that we speak about music, allow me to talk about how good English music is! I think we would all agree that music touches the heart and soul. And I believe that we all would also agree when I say that English music culture is magnificent.

I knew the latter before I came, when I was living in Spain, but it is not until you live here that you realise how important music has been, and still is, in the popular culture of the country.

Football is absorbed as part of national culture here, and renowned writers, film directors and music artists have no qualms about openly discussing their footballing allegiances.

I am fascinated by the strong bond between music and English football, as seen by the huge range of songs that can be heard at the stadiums. You can sense it in the little details. Every time we play a game at Old Trafford, the playlists that are the sound of the stadium before the kick-off and at half-time are full of great tunes. It's fantastic.

The lists, which always ooze quality, are put together with great care and even better taste, interspersing current hits by named local bands with classics by legendary groups such as The Kinks and Rolling Stones. When we take to the pitch, the Old Trafford tannoy system is always belting out 'This is the One' with the unmistakable voice of Ian Brown, a love song that has become an unofficial Manchester United anthem.

But music culture isn't only present in football, it transcends every custom in this country. For example, when my family visited me last Christmas, my uncle Luis, who is a huge fan of rock music history, was amazed by the musical repertoire leading up to Big Ben chiming to ring in the New Year which is broadcast on the BBC annually. "What's all this!?" he asked me astonished, before admitting that it was the best music he had heard at a New Year's Eve event anywhere.

The number of bands throughout music history that have their beginnings and roots in England is simply incredible.

That's why, English people's hearts and souls have been enriched year after year by the extraordinary music that this country has been able to produce, taking its musical culture to a different level. During the last eight years, I've been lucky enough to experience it first hand.

Getting back to the town, I soon realised that Manchester was much more colourful, buzzing and entertaining than the image of it that people had painted to me. Being honest, most had told me things such as "there isn't a lot to do," "the weather is worse than here," etc. etc., so my expectations weren't high. I assumed that I would live in a city with not a lot more to do other than playing football. Then I got to know Manchester a bit better, and realised I was quite wrong by assuming that.

The city centre is relatively small, meaning you can easily walk around it. Deansgate is the main artery of the town, full of restaurants, bars and shops (I have a special relationship with one of them, as my dad, another curious soul, owns an independent restaurant there called *Tapeo And Wine*, where I, of course, often go to enjoy the taste of my homeland – who wouldn't).

Then you also have streets like King Street, Market Street and Oxford Street, very alive and busy. Manchester Art Gallery, The John Rylands Library, The Opera House, The Witworth Gallery, The Bridgewater Hall, Science and Industry Museum, The Manchester Arena, Manchester Central Library, HOME, The National Football Museum . . . who said there is not a lot to do in Manchester?!

I don't work for the Manchester official tourism office (yet!) but I disagree. Then there are other interesting areas, such as the Northern Quarter and Ancoats, alternative cultural hotspots where you can find, apart from creative and fun people, magazine and bookshops, clothes shops, galleries, cafés and bars with live music – among many more cool places. It reminded me of Shoreditch in London and Malasaña in Madrid, where that creative buzz is constantly present, where you feel there is always something going on and somewhere worth going to.

As soon as I arrived, I could see that Manchester was engaged in a process of near constant evolution and growth that still exists nowadays. The city is growing by leaps and bounds. It feels young, dynamic, on the up. That doesn't just go for Manchester, the city, but also in areas such as Chorlton and West Didsbury, or small towns like Lymm, Knutsford, Altrincham or Wilmslow, all close to my home.

Manchester also allowed me to adopt a more relaxed lifestyle, without having to deal with the enormous distances involved in London. Then there was the novelty of living in the countryside, surrounded by nature, when I had always been more of an urban kind of person, having lived in provincial cities like Oviedo and Valencia, then big capitals like Madrid and London. This was a new experience for me, one that I'm certainly enjoying a great deal.

My second home

Of course, living in England has differences to living in Spain, but when you're a nomad, you shouldn't expect others to adapt to you.

I don't think it's positive to try and create your own bubble to preserve all the customs from the place you come from, as if you hadn't moved countries. There are players, talking about football now, who don't adapt and attempt to reproduce their usual environment abroad. I've known a few.

It can even work in some cases, but from my point of view it is not an ideal situation. I respect that, but that simply isn't me. I was captivated by British culture and English football from day one.

I understand that your professional ability may be so great

that you're immune to everything around you. I, however, feel better when I'm involved with what's around me. I'm also convinced it's helped me as a player.

My ability to settle surely has contributed to my doing well on the pitch; but doing well has also helped me to settle, as everything started on the right foot from the beginning. I scored on my Chelsea debut, a 3-1 win over Norwich in August 2011, which was a real confidence booster. The best one I could have, to be honest.

I had arrived a few days before the transfer window shut, having spent the whole of pre-season with Valencia. I landed in London on a Wednesday or Thursday and barely had time to take part in two training sessions before making my Stamford Bridge debut that very weekend, three games into the Premier League campaign. I came off the bench in the second half against Norwich . . . and scored in stoppage time. What. A. Day. The best possible scenario I could have imagined. So, right there, my adventure in English football had started.

I am now in my eighth season in this country, which is quite a considerable time in a football career, and means that I have been playing in England professionally for longer (double!) than I have played in Spain, where I spent four years in the top flight with Valencia.

Not once have I felt that my surroundings here had weakened or inhibited me as a professional. I've experienced short periods of disappointment due to results, of course, but at no point has the thought run through my head that I had taken a wrong step when I came to England. Honestly, I've had no reason to regret my choice. On the contrary, I feel privileged that I've learnt another language (kind of) and discovered a different culture. It has definitely helped me, too, in a personal way: I developed as a person as well as a player. I am really grateful to England and to you all.

Babel FC

First of all, let's speak in plain English here. Just like in the story of the Babel Tower, communication is key in human relationships. As I say, I've (kind of) learnt a language that I thought I knew well when I arrived here. I was wrong.

As is often the case for Spaniards who move to England, I realised that everything I had been taught at school wasn't much use and I had to knuckle down to improve my everyday English. I knew vocabulary yes, I knew verbs, yes, but I didn't know that well how to combine them without hesitating.

Also, I found it very hard to understand English people speaking between themselves (I still do if the accent is quite complicated). I remember listening to John Terry and Frank Lampard in the Chelsea dressing room and, forgive the pun, frankly, I couldn't understand a bloody word! I'd look at them and guess as much as I could from their body language. Whenever they spoke to each other, it was with such a strong Cockney accent that I had no chance of joining the conversation . . .

Chelsea, thank goodness, provided me and my dear friend Oriol Romeu with a teacher called Peter Clark who helped us out considerably, a delightful man who also taught English to many other foreign footballers and managers. He tutored us quite a few times per week at the Chelsea training ground in Cobham. They were very funny lessons. We made good progress and, quite quickly, no longer felt too embarrassed to conduct interviews in English.

I also watched the original versions of films and television series at that time, such as 'Mad Men', 'Suits' and 'The Americans' with subtitles in English, allowing me to visualize the words that I was hearing. It was a simple tool that contributed greatly to my improvement, and not just as an English speaker.

There's a domino effect at work here. When you can communicate better, you get better at your job, and you grow as a person too, which makes you better at communication, at your job and so on. A virtuous circle if you will. Languages can change your life.

More and more of us understand this need, I think. Just a few years ago, it was very rare that any member of the Spanish national team squad would dare to speak in the mixed zone in a foreign language.

Nowadays, half of the national team speaks English, while others speak French, Italian or German. Many players speak multiple languages thanks to football, with the huge benefit of bringing up their children so that they are genuinely bilingual. There are worse things to pass on to your children, aren't there?

But English is not the only way to communicate with others in a multi-cultural environment. You create the necessary trust between players to make things work. To move together towards the same objectives.

It does not matter where you are from and how your journey has been, in Babel FC, we all speak the language of football: the universal language of the ball.

'Matamundi'

There are many reasons why I feel so grateful towards football. One of the most important ones is how it has made it possible for me to travel.

Thanks to it, I have an amazing, priceless collection of memories in so many countries. In fact, separating football from travel is impossible for me.

There are experiences I'll never forget in destinations like the following . . .

– Poland. The Under-19 championships final in 2006, when we beat Scotland.

– Canada. The 2007 Under-20 World Cup. A 4-2 victory against Brazil in extra time.

– Netherlands. Also in 2007, experiencing my first pre-season tour with Valencia.

– South Africa. The World Cup final. No words needed . . .

– Copenhagen. The 2011 Under-21 European Championships final in Denmark, another title for Spain.

– Munich. That night. No need to add to that.

– Kiev. The 2012 Euros final against Italy. I scored the last goal, what a night . . .

– Japan, six months later, to take part in the FIFA Club World Cup. The semi-final in which I scored . . . I loved it there.

– Amsterdam, the year after that, another European final when Chelsea beat Benfica to win the Europa League.

– Brazil. Our visit for the Confederations Cup, also in 2013, where I had the chance to play at the Maracana.

– Stockholm, in 2017, a second Europa League trophy, but with Manchester United this time.

Even the pre-season tours, which can be tiring, what with the training, jet-lag and and thousands of miles on a plane, are something enjoyable for me. Come on, two weeks in LA isn't that bad!

Even our trip to China in July 2017, which wasn't the best in terms of preparation – as we couldn't play one of the two programmed games – is something I look back on fondly: it was, for example, the first time I'd set foot in this particular country.

And it was, of course, thanks to football. No surprise.

THE DRESSING ROOM

'For the strength of the pack is the wolf, and the strength of the wolf is the pack' – Rudyard Kipling

I f you ask any player about the most special place in any training ground, they will tell you it's our 'sacred' place: the dressing room. Our refuge from the outside world. Where we have conversations, jokes, sometimes discussions. Where we exchange opinions about football and life, where we put music on and some dance. Where our meetings take place.

The dressing room is the place in which we players feel comfortable, and where we feel reluctant to admit outside visitors. Not many people normally get into the players' dressing room, other than the staff that work with us on a daily basis.

A dressing room in professional football is much more

than a physical place – it's a mix of personalities, cultures, languages. It really is a nice experience to be part of, it enriches you as a person.

But let's start at the beginning, when the dressing room was the place where me and my friends used to get changed and feel excited about playing football.

In those early dressing rooms, video games (something that still features later down the line) and jokes were all that took place. It was a place in which you bonded with your team-mates and you waited for the coach, on game days, to come and give his pre-match talk.

It doesn't matter at what level you play football, that 'sanctuary' is always a special place.

Professionalism knocked at the door

When I became professional, playing for Real Madrid Castilla, in the Segunda División in Spain, it was the first moment in which I shared lockers and showers with people older than me.

Even though the gap in age was not a lot, I could feel it was different from anything else I had experienced before in a locker room. You could sense that a few people had already started to have families, they were living more 'stable' lives, while others, specially the youngsters (the majority), would sometimes find it hard to focus on the important things.

It is human and understandable that if you are young, you play for a reserve team of a great club, and you start to earn an important amount of money, you can lose the sense of reality and live in your 'own bubble'. The quicker you realise this, the better.

I've seen team-mates spend great amounts of money on pretty extravagant material things, change their lifestyle to non-professional routines, and forget about what actually brought them here: football.

Although it may seem hard to believe, that side of the game can be more commonly seen at youth level, with standout players who are starting to enjoy success and then get somewhat carried away. I have the feeling that this doesn't happen as often in a first team dressing room where there are normally players in their late 20s and 30s, who tend to have a more structured lifestyle. There can exist an even greater level of normality than in reserve teams, as contradictory as that may sound.

That's exactly what I found when I arrived at Valencia. A great mix of young people (like me) with a lot of illusion and desire to make a name in the football world, and experienced 'veterans' with many games and trophies under their belt.

It was a year filled with many different episodes that, as you know, made me learn at top speed. In the human aspect, I matured so much, surrounded by so many different personalities, and essentially for the first time, by people from many different countries: Portugal, Italy, Argentina, Brazil, Germany and more. Meeting people from other countries is not just an enriching experience for your personality, it also encourages you to make an extra effort to open yourself to others. It opens your mind.

I came across some fantastic people at Valencia. There were many fathers and husbands who perceived football as something natural, something they excelled at and which they had been doing for years. The novelty factor of starting to earn serious money had worn off, thankfully, and with it the thinking about what to get and what not to get. The majority were not the sort of people to obsess over what type of clothing they wore and the brand that a certain friend had chosen. As the years pass by, you rise above all that. Another type of normality sets in.

Also in Valencia, I realised that you don't have to be best friends to give everything for each other on a football pitch. There were great friendships between us, of course, but there was also the normal friction that sharing the dressing room with the same people for a long time can also create. Not once was this something that affected our performances. Professionalism is above any potential personal issue between players. I've always remembered that since then.

Becoming the outsider

The first day I arrived at Cobham, the training ground of Chelsea FC, I could not have expected a better welcome.

The team was not there, as they had a day off, but I was discovering my new surroundings, being introduced to André Villas-Boas and all the staff that worked with us on a daily basis.

I was on my way to the dressing room when I bumped into Petr Čech, who was injured at the time and who had just finished a rehabilitation session . . .

"Bienvenido Juan, the deseo lo mejor y estoy seguro de que de vas a disfrutar mucho con nosotros . . ."

I'm sure it took me a few seconds to react and respond. Did Čech just speak to me in perfect Spanish? Yes, he did. When one of the most important and experienced players in the team welcomes you in your own language and with such a message, you feel nothing but happy and encouraged. I'm not sure he remembers this episode, but I definitely do, and it helped me a lot.

The dressing room which looked silent and empty on the day I arrived would soon become a pretty special place to me. The following morning, it looked completely different. As I was introducing myself to my new team-mates, with the help of Fernando (Torres) who would become very, very important for me in those first weeks, I realised how many different personalities we had in that team.

We had the perfect mix that I always mention: many experienced players like Čech, Lampard, Terry, Ashley Cole, Paulo Ferreira, Drogba, Torres, Ivanovic, Essien . . . with new guys like Meireles, Lukaku, David Luiz, Sturridge, Oriol Romeu and me, among others.

But what struck me most was the number of different nationalities present in that one specific place: English, Portuguese, Czech, Serbian, Brazilian, Spanish, Nigerian, French, Belgium and so on . . . the magic of football.

From that moment, I was not the Spaniard playing in Spain anymore, I had to integrate myself into a new culture and it made me understand a bit better what foreign players must have felt when coming to Valencia, for example.

I must say I had great help from Fernando and 'Ori', as you normally tend to get closer with people from the same country as you when you are abroad, creating 'little' groups within the team. They were really, really important for me in the beginning and still are. Without a doubt, they are two of the best people I got to know thanks to football. We had so many unforgettable experiences together. Two true 'friends' for the rest of my life.

The story would repeat itself a few years later . . . I found the same kind of mix in Manchester United's dressing room, with colleagues like Giggs, Evra, Vidic, Ferdinand, Rooney, Van Persie, Fletcher, Ashley Young, Valencia, Carrick . . . players who don't need any introduction and some other younger players like de Gea, Fellaini, Chicharito, Kagawa, Januzaj, Fabio, Welbeck and me, among others.

Again, the same principle as I had found before, so many different nationalities and personalities. And again, I would find another friend for life in David. Later it would be the turn of Ander, who arrived the following season, and he would also join that category. They are much more than just team-mates for me.

As you can realise, being part of one of these professional football dressing rooms is truly a very interesting experience, with all the differences and unity at the same time, and it is definitely one of the parts of football that all ex-players miss the most, apart from playing itself. Being in 'our special place'.

Battle of the DJs

Be sure that one other thing is common in every football dressing room in the world: music. Because, as with different cultures, there are different styles of music. There is only room for one at a time, though, and the battle of the DJs always takes place in the dressing room. You only have to sit for ten minutes and wait.

"Eh, hang on, who has put this s**t music on? David, you again? Come on man!"

That was Wazza every single time David put on reggaeton – one of his preferred styles – loud. Wazza would go over, stop it and put Stereophonics on.

Soon after, Wayne would leave the dressing room, Ashley would come in and go straight to the laptop – which is like our own mixing table – stop Wazza's session and play some house-style music.

This is warming up lads. Only starting.

The prospect of listening to two or three songs from the same artist in a row seemed pretty impossible.

Next it is Eric's turn; he always spices the dressing room up with his native African rhythms and, of course, accompanies them with dances that a professional dancer would be proud of! And to finalise the 'warm-up session' – as we are only minutes before training here – Fred and Andreas team up to play some Brazilian hits (Eric keeps dancing, obviously). Paul's turn – I haven't forgotten him – would be after training, in the 'main stage session'. 'Chiquito' Romero and Marcos Rojo and their 'cumbia' also feature regularly.

At Old Trafford and before every away game, Ashley is our resident DJ. There is no doubt about that.

Music is definitely something that brings us together, and whatever the style, it always creates a great atmosphere in the dressing room.

Morning 'catwalk'

And if we are talking about style here, we football players are known for our 'special' fashion style. Some more than others, but you can definitely say that certain ones among us have a 'funny' way of dressing. Others would call it trendy. Others, 'daring'. You could do the same trick as with music: sit for ten minutes and wait. You would definitely have a good time!

I remember one team-mate that used to come to training suited up during my time at Valencia. One other, and this time I will give you a name, would come in every day with different clothes. I don't remember him ever wearing the same clothes twice. Ever. Can you guess who he was?

No, it's not Paul, (who has a very extravagant style as you might know). No, neither Zlatan. It was Samuel Eto'o, at Chelsea. Sam never ceased to astonish me with his attire (hats, blazers, glasses, colours, whatever you could imagine), care-free attitude and extravagant personality. What a great and funny guy he is. How big was his wardrobe?

Fixing the clock

Training schedules also differ across countries, not just musical tastes and dress sense, and so there have always been players that favoured training in the afternoon (me one of them), whereas the majority preferred to do it as early as possible. In certain countries, training sessions take place at 3pm. Sometimes we trained with Mourinho at that time; maybe it was because he did so in Italy previously. Everywhere it's different. You can also see the differences in meal times. I got used to the idea of eating lunch at around midday after I arrived in England, when you usually do so at 2pm or 3pm in Spain.

The perfect dressing room

I don't really know if there can be such a thing as the perfect dressing room, but if you ask me, I've been in one. In South

Africa for the 2010 World Cup. As I've explained already, I was one of the 23 privileged footballers who were representing Spain at the biggest tournament there is in football.

I can tell you that from the very beginning until the very last day, we felt like a family. We *were* a family. We felt like everything was going our way, and, as difficult as it is, we all left our egos aside and gave our best for the interests of the team. No matter what.

Obviously, only 11 could play from the beginning, and, as is normal, we started the tournament with a standard, settled team that would play most of the games.

Those of us who were not regulars in the starting line-up could choose one of two options. Either complain and not be ready if and when the chance was given to us; or support our team-mates and train hard to be mentally and physically ready.

We all took the second option. It may sound like we simply shrugged our shoulders and accepted our lot, but that would be utterly wrong. Our attitude wasn't the tell-tale sign of a lack of ambition. All of us badly wanted to play, with no exception, from Pepe Reina to Santi Cazorla to me.

"Let's savour this, train hard and enjoy it both on and off the pitch. Let's take stock of what we're living here," was the message we kept telling one another. That was the mentality of every one of us in South Africa, without exception. I strongly believe that this attitude led us to victory.

Of course, Iniesta's strike in the final, Villa's goals and Casillas' saves were all crucial, but the squad contributed so much to that winning mentality throughout. The selflessness and the positivity had a big impact on the energy in the dressing room; this energy, in turn, was translated on to the pitch, without them needing to set foot on it, such is the strange and wonderful chemistry that creates a team.

Del Bosque, who made a deliberate effort to praise all the players that were part of the squad whether or not we had a lot of playing time, was intelligent enough to know how to lead us.

His management style meant that those who were playing less didn't feel overcome by disappointment because he ensured that we all felt pleased at getting over each passing hurdle as a group. He even said in the media that this was a fundamental part of our achievement. Again, we all wanted to play, but we respected his decisions and helped each other for the better of the team.

The level of camaraderie that we experienced during those weeks was simply unmatchable. The lack of oversized, domineering egos was exemplary. Internally, there was no distinction between who was and wasn't seen as important by people from the outside.

Nobody missed out on the informal dinners that we arranged on our days off. *Nobody.* All 23 of us would attend, even if you would expect some people to grow tired of spending all their time with the same faces and prefer an alternative plan. Everyone was there, united, generous of spirit, down-to-earth. The level of friendship couldn't have been better.

The number of trophies that players had already won with the likes of Real Madrid and Barça had no bearing at all on the squad dynamics. People like Iker Casillas, Xavi Hernández, Sergio Ramos, David Villa, Fernando Torres, Xabi Alonso and Andrés Iniesta were fundamental to the national team's period of success. Exactly that, the personalities of the players who had already gained a wealth of experience in club football by that point, both positive and negative, were pivotal. They were key.

Croissants night

I am going to tell you a little secret now. Every single night before every single game that I've been with the national team, we had a croissants night.

What does this mean? Every evening prior to a game, after dinner, we would organise informal meet-ups in Pepe Reina's room to play cards, and eat some croissants with hot chocolate together. It was great. Almost everyone was there.

I was all eyes and ears. I remember listening to Xavi, the master, speaking about football, training sessions, players, tactics . . . I wanted those nights to last forever. It was amazing. Villa telling his usual jokes . . . Reina, Iker and Pique battling over the cards . . . Capdevila . . . being Capdevila. I loved it. Sometimes, those conversations lasted a long time, until really late at night, but they were worth it – they brought us even closer to each other.

Was that the best dressing room I've been part of?

Without a doubt. Obviously, that alone doesn't guarantee victory. You need talent and competitiveness on the pitch, two other factors that we had in abundance. And luck was on our side.

If you are able to leave everyone's personal situation aside and understand that you're part of a group, although that is very challenging, you will have the perfect squad.

The All Blacks are a good example of it. Here is one of many anecdotes. As James Kerr explains in his extraordinary book *Legacy*, nobody takes care of the All Blacks, they take care of themselves:

'New Zealand vs Wales, Carisbrook, Dunedin, June 19, 2010. After winning the game, and the consequent celebrations, two of the most experienced players, one of them awarded as the best in the world for the last two years, take a broom each and start sweeping the locker room. They clean everything. While the whole country still watches the highlights and the children in their beds dream of the glory of the All Blacks, they clean their own dirt . . . '

This is just an example of the personal discipline and humility that prevails in that dressing room. They are not any team. They are the most successful sports team in the world.

Of course, we all have days and moments where frustration gets the better of us (obviously me included), but everybody's behaviour that summer, in South Africa, came from our hearts. The unity led our legs and filled our minds. The reward was much bigger than us. It really takes a special group of people to do this.

Exception that proves the rule

Ander Herrera always speaks about it with me. He always tells me: "Juan, you would have loved to be in that dressing room, among that group of people. The atmosphere was incredible."

He means Athletic Club Bilbao. But they are the exception. Just in case you don't know it, Athletic Club is a different club. Their club policy obligates them to only have players who share Basque roots.

It is very limiting, of course, but it creates a certain mysticism around the club, no doubt about it.

He told me that what you feel to be part of it really gets to you. They are friends that play football together. Just like we did in South Africa, they make plans together after training on a regular basis. Their relationships go beyond football, beyond professionalism, they are personal.

Amongst other reasons, I'm sure that this camaraderie is key to make Athletic one of the three teams in Spain (alongside Real Madrid and Barcelona) that has never been relegated to the second division. Like Ander always tells me: "They are all normal people Juan." And, believe me, normality also wins in life, despite what many say.

EDUCATION: Being part of Real Madrid was a learning curve on and off the pitch

FAITH: Ronald Koeman put his trust in me at Valencia despite a difficult start

HISTORY: Andrés Iniesta is buried under a pile of bodies, that includes mine, after scoring the only goal of the 2010 World Cup final. We all got to hold the trophy, before the celebrations got into full swing back in Spain

UNFORGETTABLE: It was amazing when we paraded the World Cup through the streets of Madrid

UNDER-21S: A year on from my World Cup triumph with Spain, I was a European U21 Championship winner and named player of the tournament – I didn't hesitate when I was asked to help out the Under-21s

RAPID: I've been fortunate enough to make a good early impression when I've joined new clubs. After joining Chelsea in 2011 I found the net in my first game, against Norwich City

RESPECT: I quickly settled into life at Chelsea, thanks to the fans, my team-mates and manager, André Villas-Boas, who was a massive help to me

SUPPORT: When Didier Drogba was down, my words could bring him positivity. I will never forget that night in Munich

SPECIAL MEMORIES: My great friend Fernando Torres and I look for family in the crowd after winning the FA Cup at Wembley in 2012

CHAMPIONS: We seemed down and out in the 2012 UEFA Champions League final against Bayern Munich but I had a feeling it was going to be our year

GUIDANCE: I had one of my best seasons under Rafa Benitez's management. When I overslept and was late for training one day, it didn't stop him talking tactics! He thinks about football all the time

AMIGOS: Four Spaniards get their hands on the Europa League trophy in 2013 – Oriol Romeu, Fernando Torres, César Azpilicueta and me

MAZACAR: It was a joy teaming up with talented, creative players like Eden Hazard and Oscar at Chelsea

OLYMPIAN: I was proud to play my part for Spain at the Olympics in London in 2012

GRATEFUL: It was important to me to communicate with the Chelsea fans when I left the club in 2014, having enjoyed my time at Stamford Bridge so much

11

EL CAPITÁN

'The true value of a leader is not measured by the work they do. A leader's true value is measured by the work they inspire others to do' – Simon Sinek

I
n football, just like in any other team sport, there have to be certain individuals that 'lead' the teams. I don't mean only managers, I mean people within the team, amongst us. Inside the dressing room. They are the ones who keep everyone together when things go bad. They keep everyone's feet on the ground when things go well. They are respected and they also respect everyone.

We all know who we are speaking about: captains. Although being a captain might feel like a privileged position, the responsibilities of being the captain of a team are always greater, in the good and especially in the bad moments. Who has to speak to the media after a negative performance? Who is likely to receive more criticism? Who is going to speak with the coach or the board if problems arise?

As always, importance comes with responsibility.

Normally, the captain, who plays a crucial role in the social laboratory that is a football dressing room, has to be able to deal with any kind of potential situations and must have experience both at the club and in the game. He/she has to be a point of reference, not only in terms of the way he/she talks or shouts, but most importantly, his/her behaviour. There are certainly many captains who are 'silent leaders', and let their professionalism and actions speak for themselves rather than only their words. I like those.

I believe that the captain must set an example and provide a link between the players and the coaching staff, in the manner of a squad representative. He/she should speak for everyone and represent them in the best possible way. But we shouldn't forget that a great team is normally full of 'captains', even if they don't necessarily wear the armband.

In fact, from my point of view, the actual armband shouldn't necessarily be a sacred object in itself. What really matters is the captain's conduct on the pitch, in the day-to-day, trying to help the team, thinking about the group first and setting an example throughout his/her career, rather than the symbolic power of a cut of fabric.

One is not a captain only by wearing the armband, one is a captain by behaving like one.

Leading in their own way

During my career, as you can imagine, I've played with captains who have had vastly different profiles, each with their qualities and flaws, just like all of us. But they had one thing in common: they all commanded respect because of their career paths and by their experience in the game, regardless of their personalities.

At Valencia, for example, we had different kind of leaders in the team. David Albelda, the first captain who had a wealth of experience at the club to call upon, was the communicative type who gave pep talks to motivate the team. He was passionate and intense, he wouldn't let you relax or not give 100 per cent in each game. Just like he did.

On the other hand, Rubén Baraja, another 'legend' of the club and leader in the dressing room, was less of a talker, but commanded vast respect by his behaviour and impeccable professionalism, which was never in question.

We also had more experienced players in that locker room, like Marchena, a really good example for youngsters and who always had great advice for all of us; Cañizares, the great and vastly experienced goalkeeper; Angulo, the silent joker of the dressing room; David Villa, of course, who apart from being the top scorer of the team was a real phenomenon with his humour and outgoing nature, always friendly, always positive; Vicente, what a left foot; Joaquin, the great Joaquin, the obvious joker, I've never laughed so much with any other team-mate in any other team . . . amongst others. They, each of them in their own way, led us; they were the core of the dressing room.

The same happened at Chelsea, where apart from John Terry and Frank Lampard, we had Petr Čech, Ivanovic, Drogba, Ashley Cole, Paulo Ferreira in a very experienced squad. And at United, later, there were the likes of Giggs, Vidic, Evra, Ferdinand (all of them in my first season), Carrick, Ashley Young, Valencia and Rooney, of course.

Wazza is the type to get everyone up for it and he would shout loudly in the dressing room before every game, half-time or even after if the performance was not up to standard. We could say that his way of leading was more vocal, more extrovert, bringing everyone together and even taking time to sit down with players individually, trying to help, making everyone feel comfortable.

If Wazza did his bit to create that kind of atmosphere in his own way, I have to say that I've also encountered other players during my career with similar attributes or styles of leadership. I'll give you the names: Sergio Ramos, Carles Puyol, John Terry. All of them natural-born leaders – vocal, passionate, intense. They had a key presence in the Spanish national team and Chelsea's dressing room over many years. They were key to our success.

Welcomes

Now that I've mentioned John, I will give you one example, the first one I experienced, of his role as a captain. It takes us back to my arrival at Chelsea.

Bear in mind that it was a complete change of life for me. I was used to the Spanish culture and football, and obviously in those first days Fernando was a big help to me as I settled in.

If I had any question about anything I would go to him and ask. I knew him from before, he was my friend. I knew he would be there for me. But one day, during the very first week, John approached me and asked if everything was okay, if I needed anything, if he could help me with whatever I might need.

"Here's my number Juan. Whenever you need anything, please call me, you know where I am." Such a nice gesture from the captain. He wanted to make sure that, as one of the leaders of the team, all new signings were settling in nicely within the team.

It wouldn't be the only time I would experience something similar. Fast forward a few years, in Manchester this time. I vividly remember my first day as a Manchester United player. Medical checks that would take forever, endless paperwork, photoshoots with my new shirt and at the end of the day, around 9pm, I receive a message on my phone.

As you can imagine I was incredibly happy, it was a fantastic day for me, but I was also exhausted. I had received many messages on my phone during the last few hours but I didn't have the time to reply to any of them just yet. This one would be different.

'Hi Juan, I just wanted to welcome you to United. The players are really excited, as I am, to see you at the club. Good luck to you! Cheers, Ryan Giggs.' *Wait, what? Ryan Giggs welcoming me to the club?* I obviously responded straight away.

'Thank you very much Ryan, I'm really excited to be here, can't wait to train and play with you, you have always been an idol for me! See you tomorrow!'

I really meant it. He was always a reference point for me as a left-footed player, playing on the wing, the position I normally played when I was a kid.

Honestly, it really felt like an honour being welcomed to the club by such a legend. He replied to my message again. 'Thanks Juan, although I'm not happy to have the second best left foot in the club now!'

I figure you can imagine by now my reply to that . . . 'Ha ha ha, no chance!'

After that exchange of messages, later that night, when I was in bed ready to sleep as a Manchester United player for the first time, I just couldn't believe it.

I would play with Giggs, he welcomed me to the club, he said that my left foot is better than his? I hope it was not all a dream when I woke up, it felt too good to be true.

Quiet leaders

When I say that I normally like silent leaders, I am thinking of some of the names that have been really important at their football clubs, even in world football, but never changed their personalities because they were wearing the armband.

They didn't need to say too much, they let their football speak for them . . . but, yes, everybody listened to them whenever they had something to say. Giggsy, Carrick, Iniesta, Lampard, Casillas . . . players like them don't really need to raise their voice to be heard. They had earned respect through their actions and behaviour. Nobody would dare to disrespect them.

Sometimes in football, and in life, silence is worth more than a thousand words. At the risk of sounding a bit old-fashioned, I feel there is less of that respect today, and less gravitas in the dressing room, perhaps because, I feel, football players used to become 'grown men' earlier than we do today.

My turn

I have been a captain, of course. Or well, at least I've worn the captain's armband for Spain, Manchester United and

Valencia at some point, and, to be honest, what a great feeling that was.

I had been a captain before, in the Real Oviedo academy and for Spain Under-21s, but my first time as a professional was for Los Ché at 23, during my final season at the club. It was only for a brief period of time, as I would soon depart to London, but I felt really proud and ready for the task.

With Spain, it happened in October 2015, when Cesc Fabregas, our skipper that evening, passed the armband on to me when leaving the field late on in our 1-0 victory over Ukraine in a Euro 2016 qualifier: I was the most senior of our players on the pitch. Another unforgettable moment. I can always say that I've worn the Spanish national team armband and though, as I say, it is a distinction that you have to back with your actions, I still feel very proud about it.

A similar thing happened during my third season at Manchester United, in a game against Watford at Old Trafford. On that occasion, the official club captains were injured and Louis van Gaal asked me if I wanted to sport the armband that night.

He told me that he believed I was the right person for the role. "Of course," I answered. "It would make me very proud."

Certainly the night ended up being unforgettable for me, and not only for the captaincy, as I scored a free-kick late in the game, and we won 1-0 with that goal. It wouldn't be the only time that I captained the club, though . . .

Later down the line, I assumed the role after another injury crisis. The manager also decided to name me skipper for a Europa League tie at Liverpool, but this time for a very pragmatic and unexpected reason: referee Carlos Velasco

Carballo was Spanish. "We don't have our usual captains on the pitch, so I thought that the best option is for you to be the skipper in order to communicate with him," he explained. "Ok," I replied, what else could I have said?

Unfortunately the game wasn't good for our side, we lost and I remember how some pundits questioned if the armband was too big a responsibility that night. What a result can do . . . I found the arguments illogical (as the important thing would have been to focus on what happened in the game) and the funny thing is that they even didn't know the real reason behind the decision: the nationality of the referee, funny or not. It made me realise, once again, the importance of the captain's role in this football culture, where it really is a big thing.

That's probably why there was a big stir when Jose Mourinho named me captain against Burnley.

Once again, there was a simple reason behind the decision. The boss asked Rooney who should lead the side in the absence of the three club skippers, Carrick, Smalling and himself, and Wazza put me forward as I already had previous experience as captain . . . That was it.

There was no symbolic conversation between Mourinho and me about the purported importance of that moment, as some speculated. Of course, if I happen to be the captain again I would proudly represent my team in the best possible way I can, but that's nothing different to what I try to do every single day.

It is true that some managers decide who is and who isn't captain, and other times there is a vote with all the players picking their choices (it happened at Valencia), but being the skipper is a much more natural process than people believe, based on longevity at a club in a majority of the cases.

It is a logical and natural step and it happens again and again in every dressing room. In football, everything that happens internally is often exaggerated.

You could compare the basic internal workings of a dressing room with any other social experiment, just like any other group of people that is regularly subjected to the tests which challenge us in everyday life.

Sometimes the manager will decide who the captains are. That's all there is to it.

12

PLAYING SMART

'I do not have the advantage of a superior physique, therefore I must think fast' – Xavi Hernández

I t is often a lack of self-belief and fear of making mistakes that prevents players from realising their potential. After all, you are never going to score if you don't shoot. I admit that on some occasions I've been too much of a perfectionist, not enough of a risk-taker, both in football and in life, but experience has helped me break away from that.

On occasions, I did what I felt I had to do, without probably showing the best I could, given other circumstances. I had chosen to do my job without making mistakes, rather than taking risks.

On the pitch, the risk you are required to take normally depends on the situation and, in addition, some managers have different approaches. Some have a more tactical and

171

possession-based approach than others. Some like their attacking players to try and take risks, to 'feel free' in the final third of the pitch, while others prefer a more organised and structured attack. Again, adapting your qualities for the benefit of the team in the style of your manager is important for a player to be able to play more games and fit into the system. But it is also important to stay true to yourself. To know your qualities. To dare. To feel confident, to push your limits, and to know your limitations.

Size is not the only thing that matters

What else would you be expecting to read from a guy that is 5ft 7ins tall, right? But it's true.

If we speak about the aerial game, in which I do have obvious limitations, it's not all about using one's height, but is also (more, in my view) linked to intuition and 'game-feeling'. It's about feeling where the ball is going to fall and getting there a fraction of a second before your opponent, in order to connect with it.

Some very tall players are not efficient in the air, while others who are only small have a fantastic leap. Two examples. Fabián Ayala, a magnificent Argentinian central defender that played at River Plate, Napoli, AC Milan, Valencia, Zaragoza and Racing Club and earned more than 100 caps for his country, was a fantastic header of the ball, scoring many important goals in that way during his career. Thanks to his size? No. He is 5ft 8ins tall. But he possessed an incredible ability to jump and 'feel' where the ball was going to be.

Another was Carlos Santillana, a fantastic goalscorer for Real Madrid and Spain in the 1970s and '80s. Some of you may not have heard of him, but check him out on the internet. His biggest quality was his aerial abilitiy. Santillana was that good that his nickname was 'the head of Europe'.

The capacity to jump and the ability to 'feel' where the ball is going to go are the biggest attributes to be a good header of the ball.

If you have both, you could be Sergio Ramos or Cristiano Ronaldo, without a doubt two of the best headers in the game nowadays.

Avoiding the unnecessary

The process of developing as a player is not always about learning new things, but also learning how to stop doing the wrong things! A bad habit can become a character flaw if it isn't checked early on as your career progresses.

At the Real Oviedo and Real Madrid academies, I sometimes released the ball later than I should and was known as a bit of a hogger. The coaches said to me: "That's not what football is about. Try to keep it simple and the ball will come back to you."

I sometimes had to be told off so that the desire to show off wouldn't get the better of me. When you play for a big club such as Real Madrid and come up against technically inferior sides, the temptation is to try the odd unnecessary flick or piece of skill. As I explained before, you may win 20-0 and think that scoring seven or eight goals in the game makes you the best player in Spain. Big mistake.

At that stage, if your team is considerably better than the opposition, you don't experience real competition, but that one-sidedness evens out as your career progresses. That's why it was so important that I was told not to fall into the trap of thinking I was better than I really was. I've seen players at under-12, under-14 and under-16 level who believed that reaching a century of goals in a season meant that all the hard work had been done.

Oh no, that's not the case. Such massive winning margins don't help you improve as a player, quite the opposite. They are a trap. They're nothing but an indication of your level at that point in time. But they can hinder you, slow down your development, and change your personality for the worst.

It's only natural, I suppose, that gifted youngsters tend to show their skills to excess in a bid to stand out. You overdo it with dribbles that most times don't lead to anything and, instead, can be viewed as gratuitous provocation.

That's part of the football education: dribbling must be a means of getting the better of your opponent and keeping the play flowing. If it catches the eye and contributes positively to the move, wonderful. And when you're up against a side that sits deep, dribbling, of course, may be a fruitful tactic. If you take players on one-on-one, it breaks up the opposition's defensive structure.

It's brilliant if a footballer has the ability to do that and it helps unsettle defences, provided that he/she does so in a way that benefits the team. But again, and I'm sorry if I'm too heavy about it but this has the utmost importance for me, the most important aspect of football is knowing how and when to decide exactly what each move or situation requires, and if that means going on a dribble, so be it.

Understanding that an assist, in the process of a play, can be worth as much as a goal is also essential. Lionel Messi's passing nowadays is tremendous. In fact it's in the same bracket as his finishing, which makes him an even better footballer. He can be all types of players in one body.

Pass versus goal

There is no better feeling in a football game than scoring a goal. *Period.* For a goalkeeper, saving a penalty might come close, but the feeling in that split second in which the ball crosses the line is unrepeatable. It is the orgasm of football, especially when it's an important goal. Many times I've been asked if providing an assist feels as good. No chance. Like a penalty for the keeper, the feeling of laying on an assist is great, but it is never the same as scoring.

Playing that final pass is a brilliant feeling, particularly when all your team-mate needs to do is to push the ball into an empty net. Knowing that you've made a key contribution to a match gives you a real buzz, of course.

And then there is the assist before the assist. In a football world fed by millions of stats, this is the one that can be missed. The pass before the final pass. Sometimes, that 'pre' pass is the most important one, although it does not count as an assist.

Well, for me, it should, or at least people should acknowledge how important that action is. I will try to explain what I mean with one example. The number ten in a team sees the left-back running and making a movement in behind the opponents' defence line, and places the perfect ball for him/her where nobody can defend.

Then the left-back squares the ball to the striker, who reads the movement and is alone. *Goal.* Who would claim the assist?

Obviously the left-back. Which was the most important pass of the move to break the defence? The one from the number ten. Why does nobody count it? Stats are facts. Are real. Sure. But they don't show everything that happens on a football pitch. Or at least not all the important things. The pass before the assist can be *the pass*.

Another important aspect of an assist is that you rely completely on your team-mates. You can make a fantastic pass and leave the striker alone against the goalkeeper, but if it doesn't end up being a goal, there is no assist to claim.

Other times, you make an easy two yard pass in the middle of the pitch to a team-mate, he/she takes the ball and dribbles past three players and finishes with a goal and, as crazy as it sounds, you can claim that assist.

That's the risk of only analysing a game (or a season) from the stats. For that matter, and if we are talking here about judging a player's performance, the best way to do it for me is not only based on stats, but through the eyes, watching him or her play.

What starts well ends well

Let's discuss one of my favourite parts of the game: the first touch. I consider it the most important aspect of a move; it paves the way for the rest.

You can trap the ball or knock it on in a specific direction; either way, a good first touch shouldn't bring the move to a halt, but rather set you up to take the initiative and launch a particular course of action. A good first touch is going to make your life easier on a football pitch. It simplifies things.

The notion that good players make those around them

better because they bring out their finest qualities was drummed into me from a young age. And I must admit that I find that notion true.

Since my early days, I was encouraged to adopt a fast one or two-touch style, to play my own game and help others play theirs. To try to make the game flow. To connect my team-mates. For me, that's fundamental when you play in the hole, as I like to do, because you are the link between the midfield and the attack. When you flourish, the whole team flourishes. That's what they used to tell me and that's what an attacking midfielder has to do.

And for that, to develop a good first touch and to move the ball at pace is crucial. Zidane, Xavi, Berbatov, Bergkamp, Ronaldinho . . . I know I've just brought a smile to your face. Those players are the best examples of what a good first touch means in the game of football. They made everyone around them better. They made it look very easy. Art. Fantasy. Quality. It is for players like them that I love football. And I'm sure you, too.

The wall – my dear friend

I have also tried to improve my weaker foot (my dad was always encouraging me to do so) by playing more and more passes with my right.

I had a little secret when I was young. I used to play countless 'one-twos' with a wall for long periods during my summer holidays in Ocón de Villafranca (the little village in Burgos where I used to go with my family to spend part of the summer). I used my right foot, trying to perfect my pass with both feet.

I also trained by taking shots and free-kicks against that same wall, on which I had painted a goalpost. It was easy to score, there was no goalkeeper. But it helped me to improve my technique. I loved it.

Summer after summer I used to be there, shooting against that wall, which was always ready to play with me. I imagine that the goal is still painted there, although I haven't been back in a long time. I hope I can return soon and practice some free-kicks like in the old days.

My dad was right to say that it's a mistake to think that you'll get away with having one strong foot, when, in reality, you must also work on the weaker one. Find a wall and start practising!

Even Messi's right foot is better than many naturally right-footed players . . . If you don't believe me, please, check out some videos on the internet!

Feet versus space

"Stop, stop! I've told you many times, don't play into his feet, play into his path! Read his run and make it easier for your team-mate . . . "

That was Louis van Gaal in almost every training session we had with him. And he was right to insist on it.

Whenever you play a pass, it's a matter of playing where the ball needs to go and not necessarily to a team-mate's feet. This small detail has an incredible importance in the tempo of a game. It might sound silly. It is not. Believe me.

Whether it is to his/her feet, in behind, over, straight or bended – every pass asks for a certain direction and the right speed, and even for a specific way of contacting the foot with the ball. If you don't believe me, please look at Xavi, Kroos, Eriksen, Modric . . . they will give you the right answer, you only have to watch them play. They always find the right pass.

Two-way street

There exists a notion that certain players are the manager's favourites on the pitch. Coaches have even sometimes admitted in public how they had seen mirror images of themselves in certain players. Examples like Vicente del Bosque with Sergi Busquets and Pep Guardiola with Javier Mascherano.

Marcos Rojo told me that from their time together with Argentina he learnt that Mascherano is just football-mad, to the point where he analyses tactics and player movement to correct his team-mates during training and games if necessary. He's a magnificent example of tactical intelligence and he will probably be a great coach in the future. I imagine that when Del Bosque spoke with Busquets or Pep with Mascherano about tactics, it was a two-way street. They spoke and listened also. They trusted and believed what the player had to say.

Tactics also consist of teaching players how to analyse situations for themselves. I consider this as very important. This has to be passed on at a young age by awakening that tactical instinct in youngsters through questions such as: "If the opposition uses this system, what do you think is the best way to get in behind down the wing?"

It's something that is also shaped by experience and the problems that you face throughout your career, which in turn allows you to choose the most suitable solution.

For that reason, I think that trying to make a child understand the best decision to make is vital. Otherwise, it's somewhat similar to maths at school when you're given a formula to use, without any sort of explanation.

Preparation for a game that invites reflective thought over simply memorising information will always come out on top for me. A conversation rather than a monologue will always be more fruitful.

You can be told that you're going to play 4-2-3-1 and that the playmaker will play just behind the striker. But you also need to think about how to respond if you come up against a brick wall and need to put forward alternatives to open up the play, and how you are going to execute it.

Those kind of managers, like Ole Gunnar Solksjaer, let players express themselves and voice their opinion about what may happen over the 90 minutes.

An example: a player may suggest that if our opponents have a centre-back who is weak on the ball, we can let him bring the ball out and then press him. Everyone agrees, including the manager, as it sounds very reasonable and effective.

Other times, there might not be an agreement, but it has been a positive exchange. I definitely like the fact that players are able to express their points of view during a tactical training session. I consider it wise for a coach to listen to a player who sees the game from a different perspective, given a different viewpoint from the pitch, and then make a decision based on more information.

There are also very successful coaches who have won plenty of silverware and prefer the one-way street. They don't want or need opinions. I can even understand it. I think it's human to trust something that has been working for some time and it's also human not to feel like you need any kind of comment that can question your approach. But understanding the reasons why it can be like that doesn't make it the correct approach for me.

There is another kind of two-way communication that can exist between a player and a manager, and this can be 'not so easy'. We are not talking about tactical issues here, but about the role of a player in the team.

I can imagine how difficult it must be for a manager to pick the team, to choose the players who go on the bench and to also leave some players out of the squad, probably the most difficult part of it.

Facing this challenge, some managers opt for the conversational way, in which they try to explain the reasons behind the decision to the player. Others choose not to do so, arguing that if they have to do that every time they make a decision it could become an endless routine.

Some would prefer to have a closer relationship with the players and try to use that 'camaraderie' for the good of the team, while others distance themselves a bit more from us.

Obviously, it all depends on the coach's own personality and his/her way of leading the group.

In life, as in football, I'm the type that prefers to communicate and say things straight to solve problems. It is something that has grown on me over the years. Sometimes you may prefer not to speak to someone out of pride or because you want to stand your ground, but the relationship may turn sour as a consequence.

If a manager decides to leave me out of the team, fine (well, not quite, but you get my drift), but I would be understanding of the situation if the manager speaks with me in an honest way. What is the point in behaving like 'we're at war' if, in the end, we have the same objectives? I find communication between players, and between player and coach too, a very constructive asset in our sport. In everything, really.

13

RUMOURS

'Control of consciousness determines the quality of life'
– Mihaly Csikszentmihalyi

The following chapter is a little chapter. I don't even know if it should be considered a chapter, but like (I hope) you've realised by now, this book is not created with a rigid structure. I didn't want that. It is more a collection of thoughts, experiences and opinions that sit together. You can come back at any time, without it really mattering in which order you might read the book.

So although this one isn't very long, I really like it. It is about focusing on the things that we can control and not worrying so much about what we cannot control. Without trying to be an expert in any of the areas that I write about, my personal experiences help me understand better how we can behave in order to face and overcome challenges that every football player will encounter, speculation and rumours being one of them.

Every summer, during every January transfer window and during every week of international games, when the club competitions stop, there are new rumours.

Radio, TV, newspapers and – mainly nowadays – social media are a constant source of stories that might or might not be true. It seems like that's not the important part, the veracity of the stories, but what matters is the speed in which they spread, and 'most importantly', who was the first person to put the rumour out. Sometimes journalists, sometimes fake nicknames hidden on social media platforms, but there is always a 'first'.

What can you do as a player if someone has written something negative about you that isn't true? Yes, you can try to contact the source and tell them that what they are doing is wrong and irresponsible. But can you do it every single time something untrue is written? Impossible.

What you can do is focus on the important matters (training, games, commitment, behaviour etc.) and not give much importance to everything that is said outside. Or, on the other hand, we could create a vehicle of communication from and by the players to the outside, where nothing could be manipulated, as it would come straight from us. Not a bad idea at all . . .

Waking up to the 'news'

Here's an example. Summer of 2010 and I'm sleeping in my bed at our training camp in Potchefstroom, South Africa. We are playing the World Cup and I wake up every morning ready to have my breakfast and train.

When I turn the alarm on my mobile phone off, I feel

something different. *Wait, a hundred messages received? What on earth has happened?*

I open the message inbox: 'Good luck Juan', 'I wish you the best', 'Congratulations!', 'All the best in this new chapter.' *Wait, what? What's going on?* I see one message from my mother: 'Have you seen today's front pages?'

I open the website of the most important sport newspapers in Spain and I find the reason: 'Juan Mata – new FC Barcelona player. The deal is whatever millions and I have signed for five years'. *Eh?* I asked myself. I haven't signed anything! This is crazy.

I call my dad straight away, from whom I had missed calls but because of the time difference I was dreaming rather than checking my phone. 'Dad, what's going on?'

'I have no idea Juan, you know … rumours.' They announced my transfer without me knowing about it! Unbelievable.

It's not true, grandad

Another example. Sometime during the summer of 2016, and not long after our new coach at that time Jose Mourinho was appointed, I had to call home to calm down my grandfather. He had read that United were going to give my shirt, the number 8, to a different player and that I'd had a conversation with Jose in which I had agreed to reduce my game time to fewer games than I was used to.

Yes, you have read this right. How could I possibly agree to something like that? How would the club take away the number 8 from me to give to a different player? I know it sounds impossible, but when you are thousands of kilometres away and you don't know the veracity of the story, you call your grandson. 'Tell me that is not true, please Juan!', I remember him telling me.

I calmed him down explaining that it was obviously untrue, and, as always, promising that if there was ever something important to tell, I would call him first. He kept calling back after every other rumour, as you can imagine. However, the rumour was already out and people were reading it. Believing it or not, but reading it.

Does anything happen if the rumours are finally proved to be untrue? I don't know, but I guess that, in many cases, people don't assume responsibility when proven wrong. That's why, if things keep being like that, anything can be said about anyone. Definitely, a very, very dangerous pattern.

Again, all I can do is try to focus on what I consider important. I tried (and still try) to keep all my energy to put it where it really matters: on the pitch.

To focus on what I can control.

14

TIES THAT BIND

'Juan, if I don't tell you, then who will?'
– Marta Garcia (my mother)

My family has always been with me on my football journey. Such as the time I found out that I was going to play in my first World Cup, as I shared the news with my old grandmother Tita (how many times she'd cleaned my boots and washed my dirty clothes after training, bless her) and my dad by my side.

I don't really know how it works in other countries, but we (or at least in my case) only found out if I had been picked when the coach announced the list, not beforehand.

In the days prior to the announcement, and although I was confident I would make it, I was very tense because nobody from the Spanish Federation was telling me anything and all I could read in the media was, let's say, not very flattering

– typical predictions from some journalists, mostly with my name not included. I was tense.

There I was, on the day of the announcement, sitting on my old grandmother's couch, waiting impatiently for Vicente del Bosque to (hopefully) announce my name. As always, he started with the goalkeepers . . . then the defenders . . . then the midfielders . . .

My name wasn't announced. Would he consider me as a midfielder, or an attacker? That's what I was thinking when he continued reading out the attacking players . . . *David Silva, Juan Mata . . . Yes, MATA*. He said it! I didn't listen anymore to the names of the other team-mates who were going too.

I couldn't contain myself, I jumped and screamed, my grandmother's house was a complete explosion of emotions. I just couldn't be happier. My phone started ringing, but I was busy hugging them and screaming. I was going to the World Cup as a 22-year-old!

The boss

Just like football is a team sport, where you need your team-mates to win games, becoming a professional footballer would not be possible without the help and support of others. Friends, coaches, but above all family. They are the ones who will always be there, no matter the result, no matter how you play. They are the ones who were there in the beginning. They are the 'real' ones.

Let's start with the boss. My grandfather Manuel was football crazy. He played as a striker on his university's team when he was young, or at least he said so, but never really made it to a higher level.

Not having an extraordinary ability to play the game himself (please forgive me, Grandpa), wouldn't take his passion and devotion for the sport away, though. First with my dad, and later with me, he would watch every single one of our games, and would be up to date with all kinds of existing news and stats. He would also follow many other games, especially for his beloved Real Madrid, and in the latter moments of his life, when his health was taking his energy levels away, he still wanted to sit in front of the TV and watch the football. He watched three or four games per day.

As a proper football lover like he was, you can imagine that when his grandson started to first kick a ball, it was a dream of his that this kid could become a professional footballer one day. And as I am one today, I can surely say that it is thanks to him. I would not be writing these lines if it wasn't for my grandad.

He showed devotion and support for as long as I can remember. He did everything he could for me to make it. Mentally, always giving me confidence and being positive, and even physically. I remember how he would drive me to training and games, spend hours on call at training complexes waiting for his grandson and how he would follow me whenever we played.

Whenever he came to watch our games, he would be alone, in silence, separated from the rest of the crowd (the crowd was mostly our families and friends, not many people), enjoying the action. He loved it.

When I say that he did *everything* he could to support me, I mean that he would drive for hours and hours just to come and watch a game and then go straight back home.

I remember especially one episode, when I was 15 years old playing for the Real Madrid academy against Atlético de Madrid away. The derby.

He was, of course, living in Asturias at the time, but he had turned up at Cerro del Espino, Atletico's training ground, only to go back to Oviedo that same day in time for work the next morning. He only called me the day before and said: "Juan, I am going to go tomorrow to see you play. It is a great game, a derby, please make sure you will make me enjoy it!"

Luckily, I managed to score a couple of goals and I obviously dedicated them to him. I looked for him in the stands and he was, as always, in the corner. Alone. Smiling and clapping. His proud expression watching his grandson playing will always be in my mind. "For youuuuu," I screamed running and pointing towards him. I suppose it helped the journey back go a bit quicker.

He was a man of grace and style in his manner and his dress, too. He always had a handkerchief carefully placed in his jacket, always looking very smart, always with his cigar and his elegant walk. He was an extrovert type, with the right words for everything and everyone. He socialised a lot in Oviedo, where he knew many people, and he would always speak about his grandson. He always defended me, of course, against some critics . . . because that's what grandparents do, right? For him, I was the best player in the world. Period.

He was that charismatic that he would sometimes appear on radio programmes where he was interviewed, speaking about me and football in general. He was, as you can imagine, a very, very important figure for me, and certainly influenced who I am today.

Very few things thrilled me as much as seeing my grandfather take pleasure from watching his happy grandson play football and win trophies. World Cup, Champions League, European Championship, who would have thought it, eh, Grandpa? The biggest gift that football has given me is the ability to make the people I love happy and proud. To be able to 'give life' to my Grandpa. He will be forever with me.

Roots

Parents are undoubtedly key to the transmission of values that shape us as people; those values are shaped by the way that they were brought up by their own parents. My grandparents on both sides started everything. They are the unifying force which laid the foundations for my family, partly because, perhaps, they had so many children to bring up.

My mother was one of five, while my father was one of four. The most important value that I've inherited from my grandparents through my parents is respect for others. They always insisted that I should be kind, that I should always respect the people around me and not look down on people because of my privileged position, while enjoying what I did and feeding my curiosity to learn new things.

I have great memories of my grandparents from my childhood. I would spend many hours at their homes as we would always go to see them at weekends.

My paternal grandfather passed away when I was a child, but I know he was a very important figure for my family and especially for my dad. He always speaks about him. My two grandmothers, thankfully, are still with us, and I try to stay in regular contact with them despite the distance.

Sometimes normal calls, sometimes video chat, but always long conversations.

They never stop asking things, commenting on things and remembering stuff. They are very funny. Back in the day, they used to help my parents by washing my training gear and boots, as we normally trained and played on muddy pitches. As is the case with other players' family members, they also lovingly collected newspaper cuttings about me over the years. And I mean *many* years. They both have an unmatchable collection. They look after them fondly. How nice is that?

My grandmother on my dad's side makes sure she knows at what time my games are every week so she can light some candles at the same time as we are playing, which, in her eyes, 'will bring me good luck.' Who am I to doubt it?

My grandmother on my mother's side, whenever we speak about football, always has the same 'advice' for me: "Get nearer to the goal so you will be able to score more! Why don't you do that? It's simple! I don't understand it." She has a point, right?

I am so grateful for everything they did and still do for me. I am very lucky to have them in my life.

The worriers

If my family are the people who enjoy my good moments the most, they are also the ones who suffer the most when I experience bad ones, even more so than me.

I've gradually learnt how to cope with tough moments myself. Although it's not easy, I try to put things into perspective and do what I can to make sure they don't affect me for long, so I wake up the next day ready to go again. They, on the other hand, are normally more aware than I am of what is published in the press, criticism, etc. They worry more.

As you can imagine, being separated from them at 15 was definitely one of the toughest times of my life, a difficult experience for all of us because of the uncertainty around how I would react to such a change and the palpable fear linked to such a huge decision that could go badly wrong.

In some ways, that worry never quite faded away. It's understandable, perhaps inevitable.

For example, when I wasn't getting game time at Valencia and was about to be sent out on loan it was like torture for them. They feared that my first taste of professional football had turned sour, and they were incredibly relieved when Ronald Koeman finally gave me the chance to play regularly.

Another time was when I was left out of the Euro 2016 squad. They feared that I would be inconsolable, so down. Of course, they know me, and they know how disappointed I was, but I tried to reassure them that it wasn't that bad, that life goes on, that I would keep going no matter what.

As they are not with me day-to-day anymore, they find it harder to know what's going through my head, which is understandable. Their imaginations run wild, which is why a little message or a call will calm them, and I know that.

If I don't play one day or if the press hangs me out to dry, my message to my parents is something along the lines of: "Look, just don't worry. It's normal that you can feel hurt, but don't let if affect you too much. It affects you more than it affects me – and I'm the one going through it." They admit that I'm right. I've found myself in the position of passing on that message on multiple occasions.

The call

My mother has always been more worried about my physical wellbeing during a match than the result. That's why, even now, I always call her when I'm on the coach on the way to the stadium. Always. It's a ritual that we both enjoy, and which is also an extra source of motivation for me.

"Be careful. Enjoy, shoot . . . and try not to get hurt," are always her words. Heaven knows how she would cope if I were, say, a free skier.

But for all that she gets rather nervous during games, she still doesn't miss a single one. She's even gone so far as to send me text messages during a game. She's fully aware of the fact that, obviously, I can't see it, so I imagine that she does it as a kind of release mechanism for her worry and sometimes frustration. Whenever I had a knock, or I looked slightly injured during a game, the first message on my phone is hers. 'Are you ok? Tell me something when you can.'

As I will explain fully in a later chapter, I was sent off for the first and, thankfully, only time in my career when I picked up two yellow cards in three minutes. The first message I received when I got into the dressing room was from, guess who? Yes, my mother. 'How are you? It was harsh, but you learn from these sorts of things.'

Sometimes, she even goes so far as to give me football 'lessons' (you understand now why her mother does the same, right?). 'You should've shot there. You should've crossed it.'

I guess it's all part of being a mother, and we only have

one. My mother is undoubtedly a key figure in my life. I will always do everything that's in my hands to make her happy. She deserves it more than anyone else.

Making decisions

I have told how moving to Valencia was a family decision, as was leaving home at 15 to head to the Real Madrid academy. As I've got older, I've had greater autonomy in terms of choosing my next professional challenge. I've been lucky enough to make decisions based on what I genuinely wanted, turning down more lucrative offers that didn't appeal to me at the time.

My family never failed to protect me, like when I chose to go to Chelsea in what was possibly the first real decision of my adult life. I sensed that a cycle was coming to an end at Valencia. I felt loved there, having won the Copa del Rey and made my international debut while at the club, but I also wanted to try my luck in a different league. I wanted to push myself. But because of the distance, I wasn't able to know what was going through their heads as much.

I'm sure they found it tough during the final few months of my time in London, when my playing time dried up. Of course, they enjoyed the win in the 2012 Champions League final in Munich as much as anyone.

A very large family following was with me that day, a dozen of us, the largest ever at any of my games. My grandfather found himself having a bite to eat next to Roman Abramovich, and assured him it would all work out fine, as I had won every final I had played in!

Again, my grandad being himself . . .

'Feel the grass, look around, enjoy the moment'

I had a conversation with my sister Paula the night before that game that left its mark on me. She's a person who can exert a great deal of influence on others, especially me, although she may not know it. Her own way of seeing life and her personality have always been exemplary in my eyes. I've always admired my sister.

She spends a considerable part of her life travelling, discovering the world, experiencing and helping out others. She definitely has that 'selfless gene'. She had been to Africa before the final against Bayern Munich, and she told me about the experience of meeting people who were so vastly different from the norm in our culture, that western bubble in which we tend to be so blind to the outside world.

She specifically told me about a guy that she had met and how they had chatted about our connection as humans with the earth under our feet, with nature. They spoke how much we normally under-appreciate what's around us, and how we limit our senses. Apparently nothing to do with football, right?

Well, her last words ahead of the final were something like this: "Juan, make sure you enjoy the moment. Make the most of the experience. Take in everything around you, the lights, the sounds, feel the grass. Try to stop for a moment to think about where you are and how wonderful it is to be there before the game kicks off."

Paula reminded me, with the right words and perfect timing, of something which held true, and which gave me strength. I did feel the grass. In fact, I took a bit of it and smelled it. It smelled like football, like the old days playing in Asturias with my friends, like the smell of the 'praos' back in the day.

I thought about Paula. I wanted to win for her, for them. So there I was, surrounded by 75,000 people, smelling grass and closing my eyes, seconds before starting the Champions League final. If you watch that game back, and look for me just before the referee blows the whistle, you will probably be able to see the grass on my hands. That's the influence she has on me.

Her 'world' is certainly different from mine. She studied tourism, advertising and public relations, which led her to work for an online marketing company, but she ended up following her real passion, which is helping people, travelling, discovering. She now lives in Iceland after having been in Ethiopia working for UN Women (The United Nations Entity for Gender Equality and the Empowerment of Women, to give it its full name) which is devoted to improving the situation for women worldwide. She had been stationed in Bolivia and Brazil previously. She's a citizen of the world.

I love her perception of life, her curious and altruistic nature, her respect for other people, her desire to enjoy new experiences and live life to the full. Above all, I admire her ability to empathise and communicate. She makes the most of every human conversation, no matter the person's origin or condition, and she doesn't judge. That's why I've learnt so much from her. She made me see life and football from a wider perspective, not just shutting myself in the bubble of success and fame that can sometimes claim us. Paula brings me closer to 'real' life. Paula is unique.

During our childhood, she always took care of me. She

would defend me against anything or anyone. She always made sure that her little brother was fine. I will never forget that. As you can imagine, it was tough for us to be separated when I was just 15. She is 20 months older than I am, and we had always lived together previously, following my father's travels as a footballer. We also went to the same school, Colegio Gesta 1, although she was two academic years above me.

We were very, very close, but moving to Madrid brought our years of living together to an end – for a while, as when I moved to London eight years later, she came to stay with me in my flat for some time. She didn't move in permanently, but she did make the most of long periods of time to re-establish contact between us.

We could share our days once again, we could spend time together, as we had been used to. It was a wonderful experience for the both of us. Paula is definitely one of the most important people in my life and my love and devotion for her goes beyond anything I can possibly write.

Not everything is rosy

Our parents got divorced when I was still a child. I was around 11 years old, I reckon. Fortunately, it was an 'amicable' split (if it ever can be), and they were always both present when it came to making important decisions for the family and for myself, such as my moves from team to team. My parents were wise enough to put their children's interests above their differences. Not everyone is as lucky as I was when a thing like this happens. Especially with time, I really appreciate that.

There are examples of families that get broken up because of football. Or well, because of what can come with playing football at a high level: throw in personal interest, jealousy, money . . . the connection between a player and his/her family entourage can become strained, sadly. What should be a case for celebration, often becomes an unpleasant situation. I know team-mates who don't speak to their parents. It's a scenario that plays out more frequently than you would think. And frankly, I find it very sad.

In my opinion, and in order to avoid situations like these, there are some key things that should happen. Firstly, players should feel and show gratitude towards the people who were present in their lives and helped them reach their goals. It's only right and proper to be grateful. If that was the case with parents, I genuinely cannot understand how you could 'forget' about them or leave them behind. It really is a shame.

Also, and I think this happens quite often, parents can be overly protective. To some extent, it's a natural instinct to put up a barrier around the boy or girl who you've been bringing up for his/her entire life when he/she turns into a 'superstar' – sometimes from one day to the next. You feel as if he/she's running away, while strangers you are suspicious of regularly approach him/her. I do understand that, but I consider it a huge mistake, however, to completely isolate that son/daughter, as is often the case: better to make mistakes and learn from them than living a life in which you are not able to make your own decisions. There has to be a balance.

If the boy/girl forgets his/her origins because of the success and fame, or if the overbearing father protects him/her from all dangers, imaginary ones included, that balance is broken

Money often ends up causing family relationships to collapse. I find it natural to help out the people close to you when you start earning a sizeable salary and to make generous gestures towards people you feel close to. It's a different story altogether when families ruin a player by squeezing every last penny out of him/her, which, unfortunately, I also have seen happening. And not just once. So yes, success, recognition, fame, money . . . all of that might sound very good, and it can be indeed, but please if you get it, make sure you don't let it ruin your life and the lives of your loved ones. It does happen, as illogical as it seems.

More than an agent

It's normal for people to ask me what it's like having your father as your agent, precisely because there are so many stories of interfering agent-fathers.

I always respond the same: I know that my father always wants the best for me. That doesn't happen with all agents.

He's more trustworthy than an agent who doesn't know me and for whom, when you enjoy more success, personal interests come first, rather than yours. I feel more relaxed having my father because I know that he's going to defend my interests and help me diversify my career with financial, marketing and PR advisers.

He never meddled during my childhood, wasn't excessively on my case and didn't demand too much from me, which, as I explain various times in this book, does happen in other situations. He was a silent observer who always gave me my own space. He doesn't represent just me, by the way, as he is a FIFA licensed agent who has taken on representing many other players. I do think that he is very good at what he does. I promise I'm not biased. Well, maybe a little.

I haven't encountered many problems in terms of distinguishing between the two roles that my father plays. It goes without saying that he's one of the most important people in my life, but I always try not to let our professional affairs invade our personal lives.

The aim certainly isn't to spend the whole day discussing work matters with him because we would both lose something far more important, the bond that we have always had together that comes to fathers and sons. We're both on the same page. Family time and work chat are separate matters.

Sometimes, we'll both be in the kitchen and he'll suddenly think of a work-related question for me, but I'll stop him right there. "Not now, Dad . . . let's relax. We'll speak about that another time." He respects that. I feel that I have the freedom and determination to say no to some of his suggestions if that's what I think is best. We have an honest relationship. I don't think that this is the rule in the football world. He's my agent, yes, but before everything, he is my dad. My friend. My mentor. I love you, Dad. Thanks for everything.

Home truth

This is just how it always was, is and will remain. My family has always stayed by my side, without ever overstepping the mark. They've never adopted a domineering approach in terms of my affairs. They've taken the good with the bad. They've given me the level of support I needed; they've also been frank when expressing their opinions, including the odd home truth.

My mother doesn't hold back when she tells me things that I don't like to hear, even if it bothers me. "If I don't tell you, who will?" she always tells me. She's right. Close family members and real friends can tell you things other people around you wouldn't dare to mention. It's something that I've learnt to value. It is very important.

My opinion is that a family must have the ability to teach a child how to think, make their own decisions, make mistakes, learn, and, above all, try to be happy. 'You have to earn lots of money!' and 'You have to be successful!' I've heard that at football academies, more than once, when what should be coming out of their mouths is: 'Be happy and if you are, I'll have done a good job as a parent.'

Sadly, such sentiments are expressed less frequently than I would like, and not just in football. For being always supportive to me, for giving me their love at any time, for telling me the truth no matter what, and for bringing me up the way they did, I will always be grateful and thankful to my family.

Without you, I wouldn't be who I am, neither would I be writing this. Thanks from the bottom of my heart. Thanks for allowing me to make my dreams come true.

I love you all.

15

EL MISTER

'We, by position, feel above them, but we are below. We depend on them' – Coach Julio Velasco (speaking about the importance of managers in teams and their relation to the players)

'Lads, meeting tomorrow at 10.45am before training.' We always watch videos of our rivals. It is a vital part of the plan. We analyse how they might play, their weaknesses and also their qualities, so we have a better picture of the opponent we are going to face. It's not a secret, I'm sure every team does the same. I do think that images help a lot, as a good image is worth a thousand words.

But there is also a risk that comes with the analysis. The risk of overestimating the opposition in such a way that can dent the players' confidence and exaggerate the challenge ahead. And that is not a good idea. If the videos are too long, players can also lose concentration.

El Mister (what we call 'the boss' in Spain) Ole Gunnar

Solskjaer does it in such a way that gives you the necessary information about the opponents, but makes you feel that you can explore their weak spots and beat them. No matter who they are. I find that a very wise way to face a game.

We have a team of people always on this kind of information, editing the videos and trying to simplify everything into a few key points, and they are definitely a great help for all us players. Also, if you are the type of player who likes to re-watch the games and analyse what was done right and ways it can be improved, they supply you with the videos and editings. So, we have many various ways of trying to improve performances and to keep on learning, and I think it's a good idea to use them as much as you can.

Obviously, while you are reading all this, you can think: 'yes Juan, whatever, the theory is great, but there is a big difference between having ideas and opinions (like I have been doing here) and being in the dugout as a manager.' Of course! You would never know how difficult it is to put everything that is said into practice unless you are there. I only speak from a personal point of view and with personal opinions.

Under no circumstances do these opinions make me qualified for anything else other than being able to put some lines together, but I do have a clear (maybe wrong) idea about what qualities (among many others) a great manager has to have: tactical knowledge, the capacity to surround him\ herself with the right people, and the ability to communicate in a way that motivates and convinces the players. A very tactically-aware coach who doesn't have the ability to communicate and convince the players would never lead a team to reach its full potential.

Roberto Di Matteo is the perfect example of a coach who had a remarkable capacity to convince his team that we could win against everyone. He didn't only focus on tactics, but he knew how to get through to people and he was, in that way, a marvellous leader. As I'll explain shortly, those qualities helped us win the Champions League in 2012, when very few people had faith in our team.

A united group filled with belief is worth far more than a good system lacking motivation.

The plan

Before taking to the pitch for a game, you need a plan. Just like a chess player has a plan for every match, football managers have their own plans for every game. They have internalised a strategy for dealing with possible scenarios that could arise. And then they need to do the hardest job: convince their players that their ideas are correct and will work. Seduce them (us) to execute their plan.

Of course, you can prepare for a game in a certain way, only for it to end up going differently. It's still important to have a plan and a structure, though, which you believe will work.

There will always be scope for improvisation, sure, given that so many matches are decided by a moment of brilliance – or a mistake. Or by chance, that little and big cause (at the same time) that all managers hate. Chance plays a big part in the results in football, whether we like it or not.

Coming back to the plan, to the tactics, they can be learnt through three stages. First, you need good teachers (master); second, you have to believe that it's the best way to win (convincing); and third, through understanding and processing those lessons (training sessions, practice) you have to stay focused during games and apply what you have worked on during the week. Preparing for a match all week long and absorbing heaps of tactical information is of little use if it all escapes your mind once the referee blows his or her whistle. That's why it's essential to be tactically intelligent as a player in order to carry out what the coach has asked of you. Some footballers have outstanding attributes, but struggle with the team's tactical structure and what they need to do in their position. That works against them when the coach chooses his/her line-up, as it can be seen as a serious weakness.

I like players to be tactically astute. I see footballers like Michael Carrick and Ander Herrera who illustrate my point. They may not be the strongest, fastest or most aggressive, but I would always want them in my team. Their ability to interpret the game is a huge skill in my book. If you can't read, how do you think you'll be able to write?

Planning a football game is like planning a chess match, but the difference comes once the referee blows the whistle: the chessboard can be blown to pieces.

AVB

It's 2011. A young, brave manager was determined to lead the way at Chelsea and win trophies in style for the club. André Villas-Boas, after doing the League-Cup-Europa League treble with FC Porto in the previous season, arrived in London. So did I. I remember very clearly my first face-to-face conversation with André.

I could feel his hunger and determination to win trophies.

He was full of energy, ready for the challenge. His training sessions were a mix of small-sized exercises with normal pitch-sized ones as he tried to adapt the style of our game to his idea of football. There was a lot of ball work, too.

In some ways, you could feel that he had previously worked with José Mourinho and Rui Faria, because these kinds of training sessions had a lot of things in common with the ones I would find later with José as a manager.

Although things didn't work as expected for him at the club, and we were not getting the results we wanted, he was a very helpful figure during my early days in England. He was the manager who brought me to the Premier League. I will always be very grateful to André, personally and professionally. We would end that season in a very special way, and although he was not with us any more, he obviously had played his part in taking us there. It's so easy to forget how stories start ... and that one started with him.

Touching hearts

When I say 'end' that season in a special way, I mean – besides winning the FA Cup (my first trophy in England) – *that night* naturally *the* night. The Champions League final against Bayern Munich in the Allianz Arena, 2012.

A man who knew how to 'electrify' us, Roberto Di Matteo, was put in charge of the first team after Villas-Boas's departure. He was a manager who called on group togetherness and emotional dynamics more than on tactical issues. He got us together. He knew how to get to us.

The perfect example of his approach came as we were about to face Bayern. At our hotel, just minutes before leaving on the team bus for the stadium for one of the most important nights of our lives, he had prepared a surprise for all of us.

We gathered in the meeting room, as always prior to a game, and were ready to watch the final video of set pieces and key points. But that didn't happen. Instead of showing a video of our opponents, focusing on how good they were and how perfectly we would have to play in order to beat them in their own stadium, he said, surprisingly: "Guys, we have come to this point, all of us together, and that means not just us in this room, but also all the people around us, our families, who have been a great help in the difficult moments. I want to show you something that I hope will make you feel proud."

He pressed the 'play' button on his laptop. Something really special was about to begin. There were 25 guys all silent, looking at the big screen in front of us. Suddenly, starting with the goalkeepers and featuring every single player in the team, our families and friends were sending us a message of courage and passion that we would never forget. Wives, partners, mums, daughters and sons, fathers and grandparents. I still get goosebumps thinking about it. The effect it had on us was electrifying. It was Roberto's idea. He considered that part of the game crucial, and he was right in every respect, in what he showed us, as well as in the timing. He was spot on.

We all know what happened a few hours later, but we cannot forget that not everything was easy along the way; quite the opposite. Some people were criticising us for playing with a defensive approach in some games. Chelsea play 'catenaccio,' they said.

Well, when you play against opponents like Barcelona in the semi-final, or Bayern in the final, the best thing you can do is adapt your team in order to find the best route to victory. Let's be honest, both of these teams were favourites to beat us, and it was pretty difficult to take the ball off them for long periods. We had to play compact and take our chances, and that's what we did. Our supporters, obviously, didn't see the criticism in the same light. They were happy because we ended up winning. The unquestionable power of results.

We were aware of our own limits and so we tried to play to our strengths. Di Matteo understood that. We also produced some attacking performances where we played attractive football, against Napoli in particular, when we overcame a 3-1 deficit from the first leg.

After winning the FA Cup and the Champions League, and then having started in a shaky way the following season, Roberto parted ways with Chelsea. He will always be remembered as the manager who lifted that precious European trophy for the club for the first time. *Grazie Roberto.* He was rather different as a character from the man who would succeed him. There are many different ways to win.

Thinking about football 24/7

I wake up. Something does not feel right. It feels late but I want to check the time on my phone. I take it from the bedside table and . . . it is 9.45am. I have many missed calls from the player care staff at the club. I don't know what happened, but we train at 10am and I should have arrived at the training ground 30 minutes earlier.

I panic. I get dressed as quickly as I can and take my car, direction Cobham. I arrive and nobody is in the dressing room. They are all outside, already training. It's 10.15am (or probably a bit later). I put my training gear and my boots on, and I sprint to the pitch where the team has finished the warm-up. I'm welcomed by a round of applause. Typical.

I go straight to Rafa: "Lo siento mister, me dormí." His reply to my "I'm sorry boss, I nodded off" couldn't have been more Rafa! "Juan, they play with two tall centre-backs, so try to get in between the lines and feed the striker with through balls. They are not quick at all. Play balls in behind them."

I took five seconds to react. What? Wait a minute. He didn't pay any attention whatsoever to my apology; all he was bothered about was my role in the next game. I was saying sorry for being late to training and he was talking about how to hurt the rival at the weekend when we had the ball in their half of the pitch. All that ran through his head was football, football and more football.

He was certainly aware that I had arrived late, but he decided to put it aside for the time being, all because of his relentless dedication to his job. That episode epitomises Rafa Benítez.

He breathes football. He even lived five minutes away from the training ground, where he spent most of the day, every day. Later, in Madrid, they told me he actually lived in the training ground. He analyses every opponent in astonishing detail. And he speaks about it at all times; in the middle of a lunch, moving water bottles, napkins, or the salt and pepper pots as if they were the next opponents' defensive line; in the middle of a long flight to Japan, using pillows and blankets as their strikers; or when you are apologising for being 15 (or maybe a bit more) minutes late for training.

That's Rafa, thinking about football 24/7.

I remember how we started doing passing, positional and finishing drills on Rafa's very first day at Chelsea. It surprised some, but made sense to me, because he wanted to leave his imprint on the team from the word 'go'. Later in the season, we would end up winning the Europa League for the first time in the club's history. Yes, he faced some difficulties on the way, but the end was not bad, not bad at all.

Although he may not always seem it, Rafa is another coach who can be very close to his players, someone who gave me a lot of confidence through our conversations, and whom I felt very close to.

As much as I understand that there has to be a certain distance between a leader and his/her group, I really appreciate coaches who, for example, share anecdotes from their playing careers, their early days in the dugout, and speak with the players about other different matters.

Rafa does that a lot and I enjoyed listening to him. Mourinho, Villas-Boas, Unai Emery and Solksjaer, for example, are other managers that do the same.

'Welcome to the biggest club there is'

The first time I met David Moyes was seconds after coming out of a helicopter, as this is how I arrived at Manchester United's AON Training Complex. Pretty cool, I know. Bond-style.

He was waiting for us to land and welcomed me and my family with a big smile and these words: "Welcome to a fantastic club, a massive club. The biggest club there is."

Then he took us to his office and we talked. "Juan, I know what type of player you are, I know what you can bring to the team. I need a player like you who can link the play."

It certainly had to be difficult to replace a figure like Sir Alex Ferguson, the most successful manager in football's history. It was impossible, in fact. When I arrived, late January, the campaign was already halfway gone and things were not going too well. We were seventh in the league. Results were not materialising and the atmosphere was not ideal. A few months later, after some more disappointing games, the club decided to part with Moyes and chose Ryan Giggs to look after the first team until the end of the season. The David Moyes era had been much, much shorter than expected.

Just like André at Chelsea, he tried his best, as he is a committed and dedicated manager, but we were just not performing well and results were not good enough. Even at his farewell, he showed integrity and said goodbye to us in a very classy way, shaking all our hands and looking us all in the eye, wishing us good luck for the future. I made sure to thank him for bringing me here and wished him all the best. Again, I felt sorry for the man who was leaving, feeling partly responsible as every player does when a decision like this is made. Ryan took charge for a few games, and during the summer the club announced our new manager. Another with plenty of experience in the game.

'Please, introduce yourself'

"Hi, I'm Louis van Gaal, please can you introduce yourself and tell me things about you?" The manager, Ryan Giggs, myself and a bottle of Rioja wine (which he suggested we should try) were in that room. It was pre-season, in Los Angeles, and I was about to 'introduce myself' to my new coach.

Those who know Van Gaal know how intimidating he can

be face to face. *Things about myself?* I thought. *What does he mean?* I didn't know where to start. I took the safe route.

"My name is Juan, I am 26 and I've been playing football since I've had a memory . . . "

"I know that," he interrupted. "Tell me about your personal life. Do you have a wife? Children? What do you like apart from football?"

And so he started firing off direct questions about my life and career before moving on to footballing matters. "Where do you think you can play? What's your position? Where do you see yourself in this system?"

It was the first time we had been face to face and the situation couldn't have been much more of a shock. He wanted to get to know the player and the person, too.

It was, also, a two-on-one in a matter of minutes. Not only did I have to answer my questions, but I also had to translate Antonio Valencia's responses because the manager felt that he would express himself better in Spanish, a language that he, Van Gaal, speaks very well thanks to his two spells at Barcelona – but I had to play the interpreter for Giggs. Antonio is a very shy guy and I imagine that having me by his side helped him, even more so in such a surreal situation.

Louis wanted to see what we were made of and how we reacted through his interrogation. Obviously, he only had good intentions and simply wanted to get to know his players better on and off the pitch.

The frightening aura around him soon dissipated to reveal a kind-hearted man. We started to notice how emotional he would get during his briefings. When we had played very well or covered more ground and had more chances than the opposition, you could see the spark in his eyes, portraying how moved he was by his players' effort.

He would also tell us about how he had received a letter from a mother thanking him because three players had stopped to sign autographs for her children after waiting for us for hours outside the training ground. He was genuinely moved by those small details.

Van Gaal, indeed, took a keener interest in the player's human side than in his footballing ability. He stressed the importance of stopping to speak to fans at any time and not wearing hats or extravagant attire. That probably came from his interactions with children during his time as a PE teacher. Behind that strong appearance, there was a much softer side to him.

On the pitch, he had a very special style of training that was structured in a rather routine manner. You were clear about what you were going to do before each session, which drills you would be doing and how you would prepare for games. He really liked getting us to play on the deck and only opting for long balls as a last resort, rather than it ever being the team's plan A. His preference was for us to bring the ball out and play a passing game.

Off the pitch, he was also very structured in matters like all of us having lunch together at the training ground. We divided ourselves into tables and had to wait for one table to finish picking their food before we could pick ours. When we travelled, whoever was one minute late was handed a not insignificant fine. He believed marketing appearances were an important part of our duties with the club while he delivered exhaustive video analysis of our games on every post-match day. These are just a few examples. I could give many more. He had a very strong personality, as I said, and the way he communicated could be intimidating, but also commanded respect, not just in players, but also in journalists and others.

When the situation became complicated and he was starting to be questioned in the media, he remained very honest to himself and his methods and never showed any signs of weakness.

At the end of his time at the club, on his 'farewell' (at that moment neither him nor us knew for sure that he was going to be fired) he let his emotional side take over and opened himself very honestly to us: "I don't know if I'm going to be here next season, but I want to tell you anyway how proud I am of every single one of you. We fought together in adversity and we ended up lifting this special trophy. That is something that nobody will be able to change. Thank you to all of you."

We had just won the FA Cup minutes earlier and he was saying 'goodbye and good luck'. He handed out pieces of paper to each of us with our return date on it, as he had organised the pre-season for next July. We all knew (so did he) that this was a routine process, going through the motions, because there were already so many rumours of him being sacked. Yes, only minutes after lifting the FA Cup trophy. They would end up being true.

When you see a person of his age, with so much experience, speak in such a way, it's inevitable for players to feel a shiver run down their spine. A few moments earlier, a feeling came over me to do something which came from the heart when we were in the Royal Box at Wembley.

We had just lifted the cup and Van Gaal was only a few

metres away. We were all passing the trophy around and I realised it wouldn't get to him unless somebody gave it to him. He didn't want to take it by himself. He was waiting.

David and I went over to him and handed him the trophy. "Come on, boss, take it," we said to him. We all knew what he had been through, the criticism he had been subjected to and the number of times he seemed to be getting kicked out of the club. You could feel how much it meant to him to lift that trophy. He took it and proudly showed it to our fans, who remained at their seats in the half-empty Wembley.

You could see the emotions in his face. He deserved it. He is a good and honest person.

José

Louis was gone and rumours about José Mourinho being appointed as Manchester United's new manager acquired a life of their own. A few days later, the rumours had become fact. Mourinho was my manager again. And, despite the concern of my family, friends and many people, I was determined to face the situation as I'd always tried to: positively.

As expected, so many stories came out again in the press. I had no possible future at the club. I had already agreed to leave. Far too many people believed the information was true, again, and reached the conclusion that I had no future under him. José and I were together at Chelsea before, of course, and after having being together for sixth months, my career would take a different direction: Manchester.

Yes, I didn't enjoy as much playing time as I would have loved to or was used to during those sixth months, but I never had a personal problem with José.

Naturally, people assumed that the story would repeat itself. I was determined it wouldn't. To do so, I focused, like many times during my career, on what I could control: my dedication, professionalism and commitment. Time would prove me right. If you ask me, yes, this is an aspect of my career that I'm very proud of, because, regardless of winning or losing, playing more or less, I didn't take the easier way. I didn't give up.

Re-United

Let's go back to that summer after winning the FA Cup now. Let's go back to that 'second' start. I enjoyed my holidays and came back to the training ground full of energy to face the challenge in front of me.

All of us players start from zero when a new manager arrives. The first conversation between José and me, which many were waiting for, thinking it could be the last, was as plain and normal as you can imagine. We didn't make one single comment about the rumours. Nor did we discuss the past. He greeted me normally, in a manner befitting our relationship.

We started to speak, in a very relaxed way, about Manchester, what the city was like to live in, holidays, even about a Barça match that we had both watched on television the previous day, the odd player and football in general.

There was no need to discuss what happened at Chelsea. Why would we have done so? I preferred letting my football speak for itself.

We started to work hard and prepare for the season, yet it wasn't long before everything was blown out of proportion when he subbed me in the first competitive game, the Community Shield at Wembley, half an hour after I came on.

It was interpreted by some as him humiliating me, but the reality of the situation was different for me. Humiliation is something the victim feels, and I honestly didn't feel anything of the kind.

To some extent, I can understand the fact that people on the outside may have seen it in that light but it could make sense to me, knowing him, to take off the shortest player when we were a few minutes away from a 2-1 victory, had used up five of our six changes and expected our opponents to launch long balls up top to try and equalise.

"I'm going to bring you off to break up the game," he told me on one occasion while the game was being played close to his technical area.

My initial reaction wasn't particularly negative. I mean, I was a bit shocked, no one likes to be substituted, even less after having come into the game as a substitute, and I obviously didn't enjoy it, but I managed to let the initial 'shock' of the situation go away. I looked annoyed as I walked to the bench, I admit that. Who wouldn't? *I hope we get the win. If not, what just happened will really hurt,* I thought, while I sat back on the bench.

It wasn't the ideal situation from a personal point of view, of course, but that feeling disappeared just after the referee concluded the game.

From that point on, I was happy about how the season progressed, winning another two trophies and playing an important part. And I feel proud, as I said, in a way, because my football had overcome another challenge in my career, without trying to kick up any fuss. Our relationship, manager and me, was and always has been, normal, just like any other between player and manager.

We spoke often, more often than when at Chelsea, that's true; about how he wanted me to do things in matches or where he wanted me to play, as well as common conversations about other teams, players, news, jokes . . . normal stuff. Sorry to disappoint those looking for scandalous material.

Of course, it's obviously impossible to agree on everything that he, or any other manager I had, does. In fact, it is also impossible to agree on everything with anyone, even your partner or your closest friends.

But to be honest, I've never had an important confrontation with any manager.

Frustration, yes. Disappointment, yes. Disagreement, yes. Not-so-easy conversations, of course. They were needed: one has to stand up for him/herself when the situation is clearly unfair, but I normally stood up and stand up still through my actions.

They can speak more than words.

One way or another, and obviously having experienced different situations with each of those managers, I have always tried to take the positives, even when I've gone through the most difficult moments. Situations sometimes don't turn out in your favour, sure, but that doesn't mean you have to take it personally.

Trying to put yourself in the other person's position will allow you to understand better the reasons behind their decisions, which is what managers have to make all the time. Not an easy job, at all.

The challenge

Ronald Koeman was a kind a tutor to me in the year I passed my Masters degree with a Copa del Rey title – the first I had ever won with a senior team. Having the right manager at the right time can make all the difference, just like having the right teacher can transform a middling pupil into one who thrives academically.

That said, teachers don't usually teach a class in which pupils are also competing against each other for a place. It is impossible to keep 25 people happy in a sport where 11 start, three come on as substitutes and 18 are in the squad for each game. That is a fact. And that's a challenge that all managers in the world, it does not matter at what level, must face.

What is not impossible, though, is to try to be fair, to be honest, and to earn the respect of all players, even from the ones that barely have a minute on the pitch.

Competing against the clock

Here is another fact: we don't have a lot of time to train. The routine is set, almost never-changing, for every single week of the season – recovery, pre-game preparations, or working on match fitness if you haven't played the previous game. Week after week. There is no time for much more.

I am sure that all managers would love to have more training sessions to work on different aspects but the amount of games in our busy schedule makes it impossible. In England, once the season starts, for most teams, it's three games per week. It makes the manager's job so much more difficult.

The demands placed on the players' bodies make it almost impossible for coaches to devote the time they would like to the exercises they have in mind, to fine-tune their tactics, work on set-plays, work one-to-one on the details which are supposed to make all the difference.

We are humans, not machines. Our bodies can only take so much – our brains, too. Personally, I feel better the more I play. My physical condition improves by playing as much as I can. That's why it's really important for me to be available for the manager for each and every game.

Maybe the only time for a manager to work with the team as much as he/she wants is pre-season, when there is not a must-win game on the immediate horizon and you have a few weeks to practise your style, the shape of the team, the formation, movements and so on. Even so it can happen that there is a World Cup or international tournament and many players won't be back until the Premier League is about to start. How can you fully prepare when half of the team is not there?

As a manager, obviously, it is not easy to deal with all that, when your influence on the team is limited as you don't have the whole squad, but you still can work on the basics. Also, if we're talking now about the transfer market and preparations for the beginning of the season, how can it be that some teams are able to start their leagues and still can sign players after three weeks once the competition is on? It does not make any sense, in my opinion . . .

So, for me, pre-season has one clear objective, to be as ready as you can, physically and mentally, for the first official game of the season. And then, you get ready for the second one, and so on . . . Everything is very short term in our world. If I become a manager one day (no such plans yet!), please make sure to let me know if I lose my way – that is if I lose the sense that players are the ones who really matter.

It's not all about the bosses

I feel that sometimes, the figure of the manager is exaggerated. For good and bad. When a team wins, it is because the manager's plan was perfect; if the team loses, the manager is not good enough and is questioned. Hold on, surely there are many more things to think of before making those basic assumptions?

For one reason or another, we live in an era where it seems that an inordinate amount of media attention is focused on managers.

They can be portrayed as the central figures, the tactical geniuses, the real 'rock-stars' of this football world.

Please, do not get me wrong: managers have a big, sometimes decisive and key part to play, of course, in the performances of a team.

But the way we look at their work, how we talk of their influence as if they controlled everything from A to Z on a football pitch is skewed by a lack of perspective and of understanding of the mechanics of what it is to be a professional football player.

Of course managers are important, they make key decisions, they arrange the training sessions, pick the players, decide the substitutions etc. But they are not the last link between the plan and the outcome. Players are.

So, it might not be a fashionable thing to say, but sometimes their role can be exaggerated. I think that some managers would agree with me. Not all, obviously.

If you take a look at the Premier League, for example, everyone speaks about the 'gaffers.' Everything they say in a press conference is echoed a million times everywhere. Every little comment they make would make front pages the following day.

And they are normally judged by only one thing: results. Again, I cannot agree.

What kind of influence does a manager have to make a player deliver a good free-kick or a good corner kick that leads to a goal that wins the Champions League? Yes, he/she can tell him/her to practise a lot in training, but in that specific moment, in that split second? Nothing, it's completely out of his/her power.

So is a manager good or bad by winning or losing one final? No. The line is incredibly fine.

In my point of view, there is much more to analyse in order to judge the work of a manager, but, again, we live in a world that only seems to care about results.

Finding the fit

In my opinion, there are certain types of managers for certain types of clubs. So, to give a random example, David Wagner probably was a better fit for Huddersfield than Carlo Ancelotti would have been. And vice versa. Ancelotti is probably a better fit for Napoli SC than David. Are both good managers? Of course! But each of them, good in their own way, is surrounded by the specific circumstances (and players) that make them a good fit.

Ancelotti has had an incredible career, winning trophies everywhere he went; and Wagner initially managed to keep

Huddersfield in the Premier League, in itself a total success. This is not about comparing them as managers, but then, how do you judge how good a manager is? What is the mission of a manager? To win titles? To save the team? By all means, and great if he or she does, but it all depends on the circumstances and the team that they are managing.

For me, the ultimate quality that makes a manager great, apart from winning, drawing or losing, is ensuring every single one of his/her players reaches their maximum potential. Obviously, by doing so, you will be much closer to winning.

Playing chess

Another aspect of being a manager is tactics. And tactics matter – a lot. The football game is all about space and time. About making right decisions, about doing what the game demands. A bit like chess in that aspect: you always need to think about potential scenarios and how to solve them. That plan that we've spoken about before.

Managers have to find the set-up which will make their players better. They have to set up a structure in which the players will blossom, the system which best suits their qualities and best accommodates their flaws, with or without the ball.

And here, we arrive at a topic that is always on everyone's radar: The style of football. Play from the back? Possession football? Counter-attack? Direct football? Well, there are no rights and wrongs here, as everyone likes a different type of game, but for me there is one unquestionable principle that everyone should follow: common sense.

If you want to try to build from the back, but your

ROUD: My favourite moments playing for La Roja were my debut against Turkey (left) when I wore the oveted number six shirt and (right) my goal in the Euro 2012 final, which Fernando Torres set up

INGS OF EUROPE: With Fernando and Sergio Ramos after the Euro 2012 triumph

EAM SPIRIT: One of the main reasons for Spain's successes was our incredible team bond

WARM WELCOME: David Moyes made sure I felt at home on my arrival at Old Trafford

BIG HEART: Louis van Gaal had a strict regime b underneath it all is a sincere and honest man

FIRSTS: Making my United debut against Cardiff (left) and registering my first goal for the Reds against Aston Villa (right). I still remember the feeling of pure joy after scoring that goal (right)

CURLER: Set-pieces and free kicks are a big part of my game, as illustrated by this goal against Juventus

OFF THE MARK:
The best feeling
in football –
celebrating with
the supporters

SPECTACULAR: There is no better way to please United fans than to score against Liverpool, as I did here in a 2-1 win at Anfield in 2015

CAUGHT ON CAMERA: One of my team-mates must have done something worth taking a photo of – maybe it was Paul or Eric dancing to one of our dressing-room tunes!

GLORY, GLORY: Goals from Jesse Lingard and I helped us to win the FA Cup in 2016. David de Gea and I handed Louis van Gaal the trophy – you could see how much the gesture meant to him

EL CAPITÁN: When Wayne Rooney was missing from the team, he suggested I should take the captaincy. For me, being a captain is not just about wearing the armband but also leading by example

FULL CIRCLE: With Ole Gunnar Solskjaer as we embark on another season

ON TOUR: The support that we feel when we travel around the world is unbelievable and that's one of the things that makes United a very, very special club

COMMON GOAL

HELPING OTHERS:
The power of football is incomparable. I've seen it first hand travelling with Common Goal. Let's use it to make this world a better place to live. Let's create social change through our beautiful game

centre-backs don't have the ability to do so, then why persist on doing it? That would be suicidal. If you have a centre-forward who is very good in the air, then why play low balls to him instead of crosses or direct balls? If you have very good wingers on one against one, why would you tell them to play with two touches? And there is also the difference between inheriting a squad and making it. Of course, if you had enough time to sign the players you really want to play your way, then the common sense thing is to do that rather than adapt to alternative types.

The ability to adapt, and most important, the ability to apply common sense to your style, depending on the players' qualities, is a key factor for me. Of course, if I have to pick my preferred style, I would say that possession with a purpose is ideal. Not just having the ball for the sake of having it, but playing it with the idea of dominating the game, making your rival run behind the ball, and consequently hurting them in attack by opening and finding spaces. And once you lose the ball, try to regain it as soon as possible and dictate the play again. That's what football is for me, or at least, the type of football that most benefits my qualities as a player.

But bear in mind that, as I said before, all other styles are of course legitimate and valid. Everyone tries to win in their own style. And it makes sense, as there are many different types of football and everyone plays to win.

Moving the 'pieces'

The capacity to make complicated things into something simple is an art that great managers normally have. A crucial aspect of this is how a manager finds the right place for a player; and the great ones can make the kind of choices which will transform a player.

Sergio Busquets as a holding midfielder (I played against him in the youth ranks and he was a number 10); Thierry Henry as a centre-forward (when he used to be a winger); Sergi Roberto, who had played as a number 8 or 10 all of his football life, but adapted well as a right-back (although this season he is playing as a midfielder again).

Others? Jordi Alba from winger to full-back; Pirlo from number 8 to number 6; Lahm from right-back to midfield . . . These are just some of the names that come to my mind when I think about great 'player moves' from managers.

A good manager will take that decision for the player, convincing him/her, and the player will rapidly feel the benefits of it. That is how it works. When a manager proposes something, and the player sees the positive results from it, that player will trust that manager completely and always. It doesn't sound like rocket science, I know, but it doesn't mean it is easy either, because the material you deal with is not statistical data. It is human beings, and they need to see that the 'experiment' works.

As a player, it is a very nice feeling when you see that the training sessions are focused on the next game, when you do exercises that will help you play better, when a balance between concentration, attention and enjoyment takes place. I guess that as a manager, it's about giving the right amount of the right information to the right people, it's about defining a balanced path to victory.

And, of course, it's even better if you can have fun in training. Some managers are really good at that. A simple thing like having fun in the warm-up or on the training ground can, if not make you better, at least help get a better performance out of you.

Managers can sometimes surprise you. For example, one day, when Mourinho was in charge, it was snowing, so, rather than freeze outside on sub-par surfaces, we organised a kind of indoor Olympics, playing basketball, volleyball, just like children in a playground. It might sound silly, but we loved it – and it probably helped more to win that following weekend than a freezing cold, tactical training session in the snow.

Then, also, you have the opposite, managers who make you go through exercises which are utterly 'nonsense' . . . I remember I had one in the academy who, when a player missed a shot in training, ordered him to do a roll – you know, like children do in PE classes. What purpose it served I don't know . . . well, probably, he knew he was going to feature, somehow, in a football book in the future!

Look at the geese

The sense of when and how to surprise your players is a great asset to a manager, which reminds me of a story I love about Sir Alex Ferguson, something which happened on United's training ground when Cristiano Ronaldo was still at the club.

Sir Alex, while directing a training session with the team, suddenly stopped the exercises and pointed at the sky. The players didn't understand why. A group of geese were flying in their usual V-formation.

"Look," he suddenly said. "Look carefully, when they change direction, all of them do it, together. Not one of them is left behind".

Players looked confused at each other.

"In football, it's the same. A team cannot win with one, two or three players going in a different direction. Only with 11 together we can win. Do like the geese."

And they kept training. And they won a lot together.

What's amazing is that the behaviour of the geese was something that Sir Alex had been told about by somebody else before. He had just stored that away in his mind, thinking the time would come when he, too, could use it to the advantage of his team. He did it. Geniuses do that.

Some geniuses, though, do not know how to communicate their genius to the world and somebody has to tell them. To have both abilities, to be a thinker and a doer, like Sir Alex, is incredibly rare.

Managers are crucial figures, too, in boosting the confidence of their players and helping them reach their maximum level. In this respect, I had a great experience with Rafa Benítez during the 2012-13 season. I still remember a conversation (another) we had in the dressing room before an away game.

He told me: "You're a great player, right now an eight out of ten. Only you can turn yourself into a nine or a ten out of ten. You have the potential to do it. Not everyone has it. You can do so much in this position (I played as a central attacking midfielder during that season). From there, you can help the team in so many ways. Keep going."

The human dimension of football is crucial, as a manager doesn't manage holograms or robots. They manage real people, they manages egos, something that, as I once said in an interview, 'is often more important than tactics.'

Of course, I speak of managers from the point of view of

a player – a player who has worked with plenty of them in the space of more than 12 years, so please let me take a little moment to explain that I have never taken a training session myself other than with kids, so I obviously do not have experience on the matter (experience, that really important thing). I am just giving my personal point of view. I guess that's what you should do in your own book, right?!

Coming full circle

The date is January 28, 2014. After a hectic week, I am about to make my debut as a Manchester United player. I'd only trained twice with the team, but I am desperate to play a football game, even more so at the Theatre of Dreams. The arrival by helicopter is done, the medical checks and interviews are completed, the welcome from the lads has been great . . . *Now it's time to do what I came for,* I said to myself.

When you arrive at Old Trafford, and every player that has played there could tell you this, you breathe a different atmosphere, you have butterflies in your stomach, you feel that you are in one of the 'must be' places in football history. Imagine the sensation when you arrive at the stadium for the first time, not as a rival, but as a Manchester United player.

The supporters outside waiting for the team, the security people, the cameras, the tunnel, the dressing room. As I write, I still feel emotion when I remember that night. Set-pieces meeting done, warm-up finished, we are ready to go. I put on the red shirt for the first time, and I go out to the tunnel . . . the same tunnel I've spoken about in this book.

Both teams line up (we played Cardiff that day), the referee and his team leading the way, and only seconds before I step out on to the Old Trafford pitch, dressed as a Red Devil, someone touches my shoulder from behind.

"Good luck and welcome Juan, enjoy this club, it's just incredible, you will see."

Ole Gunnar Solskjaer, manager of Cardiff at that time, was welcoming me to his 'home'. The place where he was (is) a legend. How nice of him, I thought, and then I obviously focused on the game after thanking him, so the situation was 'only' that, a nice gesture from a player who had won everything at my new club and who became a manager.

Fast forward some years now – almost five years to be specific – and this anecdote obviously becomes significantly more important.

On December 19, 2018, Ole Gunnar Solskjaer was unveiled as our new manager. Coincidence, fate, call it whatever you like, but that moment in the tunnel came back to my mind straight away.

After the first meeting we had with Ole as a manager, I have realised how much Manchester United means to him. Of course, and looking back now, I should have realised straight away in 2014, when what he really meant by his words was: "Welcome to United, Juan, the place where I belong, my home, the best club in the world."

With the arrival of Ole, and since his announcement as permanent manager, the club starts a new era; an era that hopefully will be successful in terms of trophies, style of play, and above all, bringing back the excitement, pride and happiness for all United fans around the world.

16

THE BIG STEP

'Juan, if you want to become a manager some day, don't start learning about tactics or patterns of play. Start learning psychology' – Marcelo Bielsa (speaking to me, March 2019)

E very football player has the tendency to comment on his/her manager's choices. Everyone, more or less often, but we all do it. It is part and parcel of every dressing room's everyday life. But that is, obviously, just one side of the story.

When/if you're a footballer who becomes a coach, you realise it isn't as 'simple' as you used to think. At all. It's the opposite, indeed. A very, very difficult task.

As Michael Carrick has told me, your head and focus is not only on one person (like when you are a player), but on 25. Plus the opponents. Plus the training sessions. Plus the media duties. Plus the decisions over signings. Plus many other things.

Your mind never stops thinking. Who do I put in the team this week? Who do I leave out of the squad? What if the rival team does this? What if the opponent does that? This player is training very well, he/she should play, but who do I take off? What system should we play? I could keep going and going. When you are a player, you tend to think about one: 'Why am I not playing if I deserve to?' 'Me. Me. Me. Spot the difference.

Let's imagine now that you have to change from one position to the other in a few hours. A whole and complete mindset change. From team-mates to players under your command. Wow. Yes, it has happened many times. You can go from being part of the team to being forced to leave out someone who was next to you in the dressing room. How would you do that? How to digest it? How to assimilate it?

At Manchester United we had probably the best possible example of this: Ryan Giggs.

After 20 years in the squad, he became our coach overnight. In his case, as you can guess, he was already a much respected member of the squad, which helped him make a smooth transition into the coaching role. He already had a voice as a player.

I remember him sharing his opinions many times with David Moyes, our manager at that time. Then, one day, after David's sacking, he entered the dressing room as he did every morning, but with a different outfit, with a different voice, with a different mindset. He was our manager.

His first game as a manager would arrive pretty soon. We all felt really proud of being managed by such a legend of the game, of course.

The end and the beginning

Perhaps the most special moment for him during those weeks arrived when we played the last game of the season at Old Trafford. May 6, against Hull City. There were rumours that this could be his last game as a player, that depending on the result he was going to put himself on the pitch to end his career on a high, as he deserved.

We didn't know if this was going to happen or not, but our doubts soon dissipated a little bit when we arrived at the stadium . . .

When we entered our dressing room at Old Trafford, the shirt with the number 11 was hanging there. Ready to be used. He would put it on under his tracksuit. Unfortunately, we were not playing for much, after a disappointing season, but we surely wanted to win the last game in front of our fans.

With us 2-1 up, and with 20 minutes to go, the special moment arrived. After warming up for few minutes, he put himself on the pitch for what would be the last time. You could feel the emotions in the stands.

Nobody wanted to accept that it was his time to say goodbye. But if he had to, he deserved to go with a win and in front of our fans. No doubt about that, and he knew it. Number 34 out. Number 11, for the last time, in.

The stadium was about to fall in. A legend was saying goodbye on the pitch. A manager was saying 'hello' off it. He was manager and player altogether, at the same moment, and for the last time at what had been his home for the last 20 years.

What a way of finishing a footballer's journey. Perhaps, the most special way. The way he deserved.

The man for everything

There are many other cases of players who hung up their boots and took charge of their club straight away. Some examples: Diego Simeone at Racing de Avellaneda, Unai Emery at Lorca and Garry Monk at Swansea. Again, I imagine how difficult and at the same time how exciting, it must have been for them. What a shock. From one day to the next, giving orders to team-mates you were joking about with or going out for dinner with just a few days earlier.

At Valencia, we had a similar situation with Salvador González Marco, known as Voro. He was, of course, a very good central defender for the club back in the past, and then, he was a friendly, helpful and well-liked figure in the dressing room. He was the man for everything. Even to coach us, as we would see.

The season was going badly and the club board decided to sack our manager, Ronald Koeman, with four games to go until the end of La Liga, as I explained earlier. We were flirting with relegation and they thought that only one man could save the situation. Our man for everything.

Overnight, Voro was named as interim coach until the end of the season. And, of course, he did the job. That was the first time, but it would not be the last. He would find himself in the role on no fewer than three or four other occasions. When the situation turned difficult, everyone would call for 'Voro the saviour'.

I vividly remember his first speech as the man in charge. We were cracking jokes with him in the dressing room day after day and then, suddenly, that morning, he came dressed like a coach: whistle, T-shirt, shorts, boots, socks up; and with an (unusual for him) serious demeanour. "It is what it is lads. I know you consider me to be a friend, and I am, but now I'm in a different situation. I am the coach and I will have to make decisions. I hope you understand that. I get on very well with everyone, but some of you won't be happy because I have to pick a team and I'll need to make changes. Please, help me". Of course, everyone understood. Everyone helped. He did the job and after the summer would revert back to his original role.

Respect is earned not given

There are also many cases where an ex-player becomes a manager with time, following a much more usual process. It normally starts by coaching youngsters in academies; then through reserve teams or smaller clubs in lower leagues to gain some experience of managing groups and leadership; and ideally the process reaches its peak when the manager coaches one of the big clubs.

Pep Guardiola, Luis Enrique, Ronald Koeman, Zinedine Zidane, Julen Lopetegui, Ernesto Valverde, Mauricio Pochettino, Antonio Conte and Ole Gunnar Solsjkaer are just some examples of that process. But having been a fantastic player does not make you a great coach. Not at all.

Experience definitely adds something really important, but seen from my point of view, becoming a manager has more to do with your understanding of the game, your personality, your ability to communicate, convince and motivate, and your work ethic, than your experience as a football player.

You need to be a leader. Exactly because of that, some coaches who didn't play the game at a high level manage to earn respect through their way of connecting with the group, and are able to win many trophies and coach massive clubs. Previous experience as a top level footballer is not an imperative. You have to earn respect through your actions, not only through your past. I do, however, completely understand how legends such as Zidane and Giggs, for example, command respect the second they walk into the dressing room. How would they not?

Could I be a boss?

If you ask me, I'm still unsure about whether or not I want to be a manager in the future. A footballer's initial temptation might be to devote him/herself to something outside the game and take some distance from the intense years spent in hotels, on planes and at games . . . but many (if not all) end up missing it, as is normal.

The older I get (and as I am writing this, I sincerely feel that I still have some years in my body and in my mind to keep playing and enjoying this sport), the more I debate between the ideas of devoting myself to other interests or remaining connected to this sport. Well, in fact, that I will definitely do, one way or another, but I still don't know how, where or in what role.

Experience and age naturally give you an ability to understand football concepts, player-coach relationships and the dynamics in a dressing room made up of different personalities, which could definitely help in the future if you end up becoming a coach. But at this very moment, I still don't know. We shall see. I won't close any doors. I will start learning about psychology, just in case . . .

17

CURIOUS

*'Curiosity about life in all of its aspects, I think, is still
the secret of great creative people'– Leo Barnett*

J uly 2007, Canada. My good friend Esteban Granero
gives me a book and says: "Read it, it's very good, you'll
enjoy it."

We're taking part in the Under-20 World Cup, and in these
kind of tournaments you normally have a lot of time to spend
at the hotel. He knew I was not very good at video games,
which most of the squad was playing, and thought he would
lend me one of the books he had brought along: *Tokio Blues,
Norwegian Wood* (that's the title of the Spanish translation),
by Haruki Murakami.

"Pirata (Esteban's nickname) I've never heard of him, do
you really think I'll like it?" He said: "Start and let me know.
You won't like it, you will love it." He knew me very well, we
were very good friends and, back then, we spent a lot of time
together. He could read me like you know what. He was right.

Esteban was already a seasoned reader – he also tried and still does try his hand at writing – and I was more than happy to let him introduce me to this Japanese writer I had never heard of. Murakami was one of his favourite novelists at the time, and very quickly became one of mine. He is very, very good. I was totally taken in by the power of his descriptions and by his ability to keep a rhythm going, while at the same time pulling together a complicated and daring plot. I was hooked. I've never had such an interest for reading a book. I just could not stop reading it. I started to read between training sessions and games. Importantly, it also reminded me of the unique joys of reading, something I had discovered with my friends from Oviedo, all of whom are bookworms, and members of my own family.

Reading is a deep-rooted family pastime. My mother won't retire to bed without a book. Most of my uncles have libraries in their homes, which I love exploring, just like my grandfather Manolo, who was constantly borrowing books from them. So there I was, taking my first step into the fascinating world of books.

I threw myself into reading from that point onwards. Apart from being fascinated by Murakami's universe and reading many of his works, I also acquainted myself with authors like Paul Auster, Gabriel Garcia Márquez, George Orwell, Hemingway, José Saramago, J.D. Salinger, etc.

I also immersed myself in biographies of figures like Nelson Mandela, Steve Jobs, Richard Branson, Eric Cantona, Dennis Bergkamp, Rafa Nadal, Andre Agassi and Sir Alex Ferguson.

Football books were on my list as well, naturally: *Fever Pitch*, by Nick Hornby, *El Fútbol A Sol Y Sombra* by Eduardo

Galeano, *Calcio Stories* by Enric Gonzalez, *El Juego Infinito* by Jorge Valdano, *From the Game to the Stadium* by Jacobo Rivero and Claudio Tamburrini, *Football, The Dynamics of the Unexpected* by the great Dante Panzeri, among others.

If you ask me, I don't really have a favourite literary genre. I simply love how books can take you away from everything else, then leave you wanting more when you finish them.

I also went through a phase of reading Spanish and Latin American authors, such as Arturo Pérez-Reverte, a Spanish historical novelist, and those two fantastic Argentinian writers, Julio Cortázar and Jorge Luis Borges (apart, of course, from the great Uruguayan Galeano).

Yes, I'm quite eclectic in my tastes which means that you could also find Charles Bukowski (impossible to say more with less words) as well as *Autobiography of a Yogi* by Paramahansa Yogananda and essays by the Dalai Lama on my bedside table, maybe not exactly the most obvious of companions. But I spend a lot of time travelling and staying at hotels, and might as well use it to further my interests, read some more – and write this book, an exercise which I'm enjoying a lot (besides my doubts about publishing it).

Lately, I have begun to read books that speak about the difficult task of understanding the human mind and our behaviour, from *Thinking, Fast And Slow; Man's Search For Meaning; Flow: The Psychology Of Optimal Experience; Legacy,* and, perhaps, one of the most interesting books I've ever read: *Sapiens.* It is a really fascinating novel about our origins as humans on this planet and our development over the years which gives you many answers about some of the most important existential questions we face nowadays: why we are the way we are, why we act the way we act, and where we are going to. Listening to interviews, listening to podcasts, and watching documentaries are other examples of things that I really love doing in my down time.

'Stay hungry, stay foolish' – Steve Jobs

Curiosity must have been an instinctive trait in me, but I certainly developed it when I was little, through the influence of my older sister, Paula, a very daring person, even more curious of everything than I am. Her questions about life and hunger to learn made her the benchmark for me. If you have a conversation with her, you can just listen and learn so much about so many different aspects – she's just incredible.

Just like most people of my age, I enjoy other common activities such as music, watching movies, having meaningful conversations, travelling, seeing different countries and cultures. You know, that feeling of excitement when you arrive in a new place for the first time, and have enough time to visit and discover it? I love it. That's me in 'tourist mode.' One of the things I would like to do after my professional career as a football player is to travel around the world, with no time limits, just enjoying every bit of it, visiting different continents, learning from new experiences . . . it doesn't sound bad, does it?

Admiring creativity

I particularly admire those creative people who are capable of doing something I can't do. And they are many, I must say. Writers who think up a story in their head, get it on paper, and manage to make millions of people like it; marvellous painters who were considered as kind of crazy back in their day, but whose works ended up being studied in depth; musicians who possess the talent to transmit emotions through their voice or ability with instruments . . . I have nothing but admiration for them.

Yes, there have been times when I've dared to try and create something with my own hands (who hasn't), be it a painting, writing (you are witness to it), or music . . . with rather embarrassing results. Some lines here and there, some thoughts put on paper . . . really, what I am doing now. I don't know if they are good or not, but the actual process of doing it makes it worthwhile.

I think it's important to do things for the sake of doing them and not only for the result that comes out of them. Actually, that may be a bit of self consolation . . . here is why.

Proud dilettante

Let's start from when I gave myself a chance to paint. One day I bought some canvasses and a stand, and was really determined to try out my brushwork skills. It was obviously just an impulse, and while I enjoy doing it now and then, the outcomes were just quite bizarre, as you can expect. I can't find a more polite way of describing it. But hey, that's fine for me, as I obviously do not aspire to be a good painter. All I want is to keep doing it while/if I enjoy it.

On another occasion (another impulse), I got a mixing desk so I could start to understand the mechanisms involved in creating electronic music (which I've learnt to really like). I realised it was much tougher than I had the cheek to think. Of course. Naive of me . . .

Also, I thought about giving myself a chance to learn a musical instrument and the outcome was the same. Great at the beginning, very exciting, some days dedicated to it, and then . . . inconsistency. How difficult is it to learn and master something? Very.

As researchers say, you would need around ten years of your life to really master something like this, whatever it is. That shows that I have a long way in front of me, yes, but they say hope is the last thing you must lose, right?

So there I was, with an acoustic guitar I got as a birthday present some years ago, trying to put some notes together. My repertoire to date? Three songs. The ones that I play on repeat mode whenever I have guests at home and they see the guitar in the corner of my living room . . . *Oh Juan, so you play the guitar?* Maybe I should hide it, after all . . .

On the keyboard, the repertoire decreases to one, but a pretty decent one I should say. I make a vow with you now, I will practice more often. I do love music, and without it, my life wouldn't be the same. I bet you feel the same.

Disconnecting from football

If we talk about sports other than football, tennis has to come first in my list of favourites. In fact, I used to play quite often when I was a kid, and I still love it. Table tennis ranks up on my list too, to the point that I had a table tennis table in my kitchen for over a year. Yes, in the kitchen.

David de Gea and Ander knew how much I liked to play, so they got a pretty decent table for my birthday and we decided to put it there. Anyone who was entering my home would see it, and would play against the 'champion of the house', who doesn't need a name, right? It was fun. Golf, much more difficult to play well than table tennis, is a sport that I also really like, although I am just ok (being kind to myself) at it . . . It needs a lot of practice (consistency again) to improve your swing, so I do need more time to play well enough to really enjoy it. When I say I play golf and people ask me about my handicap, I usually say: 'Around five to seven.' 'Oh that's good!' they reply. 'No no, I mean . . . five to seven balls lost per round.' You can figure out my level.

Apart from other sports, music and creative works such as writing or painting, I also developed interests in graphic design, typography, photography and illustration; what some call visual communication. I find the notion of expressing an idea or message through photography, logos or fonts very, very interesting. That's why I chose the main headline font for this book and designed the jacket. I also developed an interest to read and learn from leadership and motivational materials, which thinking about it, is probably due to my curiosity in the psychological side of sport and life in general.

All these different activities help me to disconnect from football and free up my mind, a very important task to try and avoid thinking about the game 24/7 and risking burn-out. We all need to reset our minds sometimes.

Of course, I love football, and I thoroughly enjoy watching matches, scrutinising tactics and analysing players, but that doesn't take anything away from the fact that I have other interests. It's important to prove to yourself that you can be happy doing other things, which probably will also help to develop your personality. It is needed for me to stay hungry for life, to stay curious.

'I have no special talents. I am only passionately curious' – Albert Einstein

Over the years, and it's something that I should accept makes me feel uncomfortable, some people have classed me as a 'different' football player.

Well, I'm not sure about that. It is innacurate, of course. From the outside, it might be easy to fall into the stereotype that football players haven't read a book in their lives, don't have the ability to have an opinion about different matters, or similar things.

Like in everything, there are players who fit that profile and players who don't. It is never fair to generalise. Football, indeed, has given me the chance to meet some people who I really connect with, and I've learned from them many good values and in many aspects.

As I always say, we are human beings before footballers, individuals with different interests, personalities, purposes, hobbies, and we are determined by that, not only by belonging to a profession that sometimes is unfairly trivialised.

People who tend to formulate opinions on players without really knowing them would be surprised in many cases. There are many interesting people among footballers.

Coming back to the beginning, during my presentation as a Chelsea player, one of the first questions I got was this same one: 'Are you a different footballer?' What a welcome.

I don't remember my answer, but if I had to answer that question now, after some years, I know what I would say: "No, I don't consider myself different or special, certainly not 'better' or 'worse' than others. If you want me to describe myself quickly, I'd rather say 'curious.'"

18

MIND GAME

*'Everything can be taken from a man except one thing:
the last of human freedoms – to choose one's attitude
in any given set of circumstances, to choose one's
own way' – Victor Frankl, 'Man's Search For Meaning'*

L et's start this chapter, in which we are going to speak mainly about the mental side of the game and its importance, talking about the body. About the physical aspect of sports and football, as they are also obviously key in the equation. Let's start questioning ourselves. Where do the benefits of professional sport end and the damage begins?

Although it may appear contradictory, professional sport can be less healthy than playing at amateur level or doing exercise as a hobby.

Everyone would agree by affirming that a person who goes for a one-hour run every morning and eats and rests regularly, has a less damaging daily routine than an athlete who spends six hours training, a swimmer who does lengths in the pool for 15 hours or a footballer who plays 60 matches per season. Also, the expectations of an 'amateur' are obviously not the same as those of a professional skier, tennis player, etc. There is a limit to what the human body can take, but where is the limit? When do you realise that you've pushed too far? When is it too late to stop? It seems obvious, the more you push, the more you damage. That's why many former footballers have never-ending hip, knee, ankle and joint problems when they retire . . .

"Cut my legs off, please!" Gabriel Batistuta, the great Argentinian striker who scored numerous goals for Fiorentina, many other teams and his national team, admitted in a recent interview that he begged this to his doctor at some point because he couldn't cope with the pain in his lower legs when he retired. "I quit football and couldn't walk from one day to the next". It's the same story with former handball players who end up with chronic shoulder problems. It's, unfortunately, the same problem that the great Andy Murray has suffered with his hip. It's a common story in professional sport. It's one of the prices that you can pay.

And it's understandable.

If I'm a professional player and my coach wants me to play in the Champions League final, but I pick up an injury a week before, I'm going to force my body to be ready, no matter what. Everyone would do the same, right? Even if that means resorting to pain-relief injections, intensive treatments or alternative medicine. Whatever would make me 'fit to play,' I would do, obviously under the existing rules and laws.

If you deceive your body, it will make you pay, sure, as two days later, the pain will be excruciating. But in a football player's career, if you have the chance to play some of those games (I remember Fernando Torres was rushed back to be 'ready' for the World Cup final in South Africa 2010 and got injured again when he came on as a substitute), you will try and take it, even though it's not always advisable. I remember that Diego Costa was pushed to play the 2014 Champions League final, but only lasted eight minutes on the pitch.

Even on a normal basis, when the demands are still high and coaches expect you to be fit as soon as possible, you can push to recover earlier than you should. We are all used to that; us players, physios, doctors . . . it is part of the game.

I remember on one occasion, when I was at Valencia, I twisted my ankle in training ahead of an important fixture. What did I do? I wanted to play, I didn't want to miss it. I spoke with the doctor, and after doing the normal checks and scans, he told me I could be ready to play as there was no important damage in the bone or the tendon, but that the pain might not allow me to even run. And it really was painful, but I did what everyone in my position would have done.

I was given a strong anaesthetic so that I wouldn't feel a sprain during the game. It worked. I played, I felt ok. But, as expected, 24 hours later, and once the effect had worn off, I just couldn't walk. We all can agree that what I did wasn't good for my body, but in my opinion, was needed. This anecdote, and millions of other similar stories that I have come across with team-mates and rivals (many more extreme than my situation), bring us to the start of this chapter . . .

Is professional sport actually healthy for our bodies? Can you be 'fit' but unhealthy on a long term basis? How much is the price you are willing to pay?

'We are football players, not athletes'

All this being said, let's accept that football is not known as one of the most hard-working sports, such as cycling, water polo, gymnastics . . .

Some would disagree, but the reality is that many people see football players as 'privileged' athletes who earn vast amounts of money and don't really need to 'work hard' for it. Well, I have my own opinion about the physical preparation in football, but as I write these lines a memory comes to me. I'm actually laughing while I remember it.

It happened at Valencia, during a season in which we had a fitness coach who really made us 'work hard.' He made us do far too many circuits of the pitch, running around the lines not having a ball in sight, especially in pre-season (hell, pre-season), that it felt like it was simply never-ending. He treated us like track and field athletes and even measured our lactic acid levels after each run.

And while I admit that having this information is good, as everything helps, I feel that there are other aspects that can have more impact on the level of performance of a football player from a physical point of view.

Aspects such as making the player feel that this type of training is actually affecting positively his/her performances; adapting to the needs of each player; replicating actions that happen in the game and build fitness levels through them; to use the ball (our tool for playing) as much as you can while building condition; to have common sense while training and so on. New technologies can add valuable data to the mix, which in the right amounts can form a multi-disciplinary structure that will help the overall condition of the players.

Of course, this is a personal opinion based only on my experience as a player, so I ask for forgiveness in advance from any fitness coaches who are reading this and think that I couldn't be more wrong . . . I surely am. I do not speak from knowledge (obviously) only from experience, but it's only fair that I give my own opinions here. *Sorry, fitness coaches of the world, I beg your pardon . . .*

So yes, back to Valencia. There we were running around the pitch again and again, dreaming of touching the ball. One day, a fed-up Joaquín (who else?) while running for the millionth time around the pitch, shouted with his usual Andalusian grace . . . "Ey, *monstruo!*' (meaning 'monster' and referring to our fitness coach!) Remember that we're footballers, not athletes!" Remember that we are footballers, not athletes: the sentence would stick in my mind forever. Genius.

Fortunately, sporting medicine has evolved considerably over the years and the way clubs are structured now makes them better equipped to help players in terms of prevention and recovery, which are two of the key elements in a player's care, especially now that the physical demands are much higher than they were 20 or 30 years ago.

The game is quicker, the impacts heavier. It seems understandable that there is a certain tendency today based on bulking players up and 'creating athletes.'

That's completely fine, as it's needed, but it would be a mistake to only focus on the physical part of the game. Where did we leave talent, technique and understanding of the game? They can never be forgotten or pushed aside. They are key parts of our game and will always be.

Always.

When the mind moves the body

Let's go back now to the 2011-12 season. What a season it was for me. A total of 54 games, including 12 in our successful Champions League campaign, after which I joined La Roja for the Euros, then the Olympic squad for the London Games. Let's say I had a busy summer.

I played my last match of that season at the Olympics on July 29 (not a game I like to think about too much – a horrible 0-1 defeat to Honduras), and less than two weeks later, a new campaign had started at Chelsea. *Really? Only two weeks holidays?* Surely it was not enough time to rest. *I feel fine,* I thought. I wanted to keep playing.

There I was, playing in three league games and feeling fine (or so I thought, we won all of them), but something was not quite right. I wasn't at my usual level, everyone could see it.

Paco Biosca, my good friend Paco, the club's medical boss, came to see me after one of those games, and with the confidence that we shared, said to me: "Juan, I think you're mentally and physically burnt out, and you know it, even if you don't want to accept it. Believe me – you need to stop. You need to have a break. The best thing to do is to speak to Vicente [del Bosque] before the next international break in September, bearing in mind that you went to the Euros and the Olympic Games, and we need to suggest to him that he gives you a break and he doesn't call you up."

"But Paco, I want to go, I don't want to miss the chance of going away with the national team", I replied.

"Listen, I will speak also with Robbie (Di Matteo) and then you can take the following week off and miss a league game. That way you'll have a couple of weeks' 'holiday' that will stand you in good stead for the season. Please, listen to me, let's do it." I agreed. "Ok Paco, you are right." He indeed was.

We spoke to Vicente and he agreed. I had around two weeks off in September, which felt weird but allowed me to switch off from the game (although, in fairness, I did miss it). I went to Asturias, then to Ibiza with my friends where I completely switched off. I did no exercise. I relaxed for a week. In the middle of the season! I know, it sounds crazy.

But Paco knew what he was doing. When I got back, and after training for a week, I felt like I was flying. I played, scored a goal and had an assist in our 2-1 win at Arsenal on my return and ended up being named Premier League Player of the Month for October, thanks in part to a double at Tottenham, who we beat 4-2 at White Hart Lane. A few days earlier I was lying down under the sun in Ibiza and then there I was enjoying the best football of my career!

What happened afterwards? I went on to have the best season of my life until that point. I played in a total of 74 games for club and country, the most of my career, in that 2012-13 season, when Roberto, then Rafa Benítez were in charge of us at Chelsea, and I barely had time to change from our Europa League final jersey to put on the Spanish shirt for the Confederations Cup.

I played my first game of the campaign on August 12 2012 – the Community Shield, against Manchester City – and the last on July 1, 2013 – the final of the Confederations Cup. Seen from the outside, it looked like an insane workload. But I felt better than ever. Paco would always tell me during the season: "You see? I told you!" He did. Sometimes the best therapy is taking a break from routine.

Ah, Paco. Paquito Biosca. What a legend. He's one of those doctors who seeks everyday solutions to health problems, one of life's genuine jokers, who always had a knack of coming out with hilarious comments when you least expected it.

He gave me the shortest medical I've ever had when I joined a new club. It was not favouritism, mind: he had all my records from Valencia in his possession already! (It was quite a different experience at Manchester United, when the tests took a whole day. Scans, of every part of my body, from the ankles to the teeth, blood tests, eye tests, effort tests, heart tests).

He often mentioned it as a joke, but I remember him asking me many times if I had sex in the previous days, because "sex heals Juan, sex heals." With his cigar in his hand and his glasses hanging from his neck, his unique appearance, and his knowledge and personality, Paco conquered all the players' hearts. He was loved by everyone.

Paco wasn't only a doctor, but also a confidant who gave me advice and used his considerable life experience to play down trivial matters that seemed like the end of the world to me at times. He was a psychologist, I suppose, a professional listener, although only with one ear, because he's as deaf as a post in the other one! I found it rather funny whenever he turned his head to one side to listen to us.

I loved going to his house for dinner. His wife, who is Ukrainian, could whip up a fabulous tortilla. The Spanish members of the squad used to go to his house near the training ground en masse whenever Paco announced that she'd made one. Tortilla time! He loved showing us his special room for smoking cigars, reading and listening to music.

Whenever we were called up to play for Spain, he would always send good luck messages to me, Fernando Torres and César Azpilicueta ahead of games. The first message I received after getting knocked out of the World Cup in Brazil was from Paco: "Don't think for a second I only support you in the good times and shy away when things take a turn for the worse. I love you, mate, even if you lose every bloody match." On the day I left Chelsea, we said goodbye to each other in the Cobham car park. He got emotional and was unable to hold back the tears. Me neither. "I've never previously cried when saying goodbye to a player," he admitted to me.

We are what we eat

Then there's the diet. Another key aspect. Good diet doesn't score goals, but good diet can help you to play more, for longer. It's one leg of the table, because we are what we eat. Good nutrition is very important for professional football players, for any athlete.

While I've never been the obsessive type in that respect, in any respect really, I haven't measured everything I consumed to the nth degree, or counted calories, like some players do. From a young age, my mother tried to bring me up, and my sister, to like as many things as possible and not to be picky. As a result, I've never been particularly fussy with food. I pretty much like everything.

When you become a professional footballer, and especially before games, you stick to what is available in the buffet at the club or hotels, almost all of which is geared towards our routine as sportsmen: carbohydrates, pasta or rice, chicken, fish, vegetables, fruit . . .

Normally clubs make it easy for us to follow a healthy diet, free from high quantities of fat and sugar. There always is, with some managers more than others (some are really obsessed with this matter), certain levels of freedom to adapt your diet individually, so you can decide what to eat.

I may not be overly strict, but I am aware of what I need. Or at least, what I'm used to and has worked for me. I always eat the same in the hours leading up to kick-off: spaghetti with olive oil and grated cheese, a boiled egg, chicken, a banana and a coffee.

It's a routine that my body has adapted to well over the years. I usually eat all that quite a while before the game. If kick-off is in the afternoon, I do so three hours beforehand. If kick-off is, for example, at 8pm, I have it at 1pm and then at 5pm I'll have some toast with a coffee and a banana when we eat again.

Some of my team-mates go for double pasta in the late morning and afternoon, but I don't really like doing that because I feel too bloated from so many carbohydrates. Maybe as a Spaniard I treat that second meal as more of a snack . . . that's how I feel more comfortable anyway.

When we play at home, I almost always eat at Old Trafford straight after the game. We have access to freshly-made pasta and chicken by our chef Mike, in the room next to our dressing room, as we start to recover and prepare for the next game the second after the referee blows the whistle. If we are playing away, we have food on the coach also straight after. We cannot complain. We have everything we need to be as professional as we can. It would be silly not to do so. This can take you to another level.

Fortunately, I don't put on weight easily. During the season, I normally maintain the same weight throughout, and even during summer time, I almost always report back for pre-season with the same weight as when I left, despite not training intensively for a month.

But all of this is only half of the story, and probably less than that in my view: at a certain level – towards the top – football becomes a 'mind game' as much as anything else.

When the mind takes over

I can certainly use myself as a case study in this respect. If we're all in charge of setting our own limits when it comes to disappointment, I admit that I have the bad habit of blaming myself too much when things go wrong. I've improved slightly over the years in that respect, but I still show it more than I should. If and when the team loses, I feel I haven't done enough. *I didn't take that chance in front of goal. I misplaced a key pass to a team-mate. I cocked up.*

It used to be far worse between the ages of 17 and 20. I used to say things to myself like, *I didn't make the difference, I didn't win us the game.* I probably let myself be overcome by an excessive sense of responsibility.

In some ways it was normal at Valencia, when I was younger and hadn't yet understood the true level of responsibility I had in the team. But there are still times when I blame myself for things that are out of my control. I still feel pain and frustration when we don't win a game, I still carry those feelings with me when I go home. I give myself a hard time more than I should, but I have learned to control that more as the years have gone by.

I realised that I couldn't take it out on myself every time something went wrong. You win some, you lose some, but if you've given your best, you have more than enough reason to feel that you've done your bit. It's ok to feel bad. It's good to care. But the best way to put an end to the feeling of frustration is to wake up the next day with an increased desire to put it right in the next game.

It does happen that, sometimes, you crash down, and there is no apparent explanation for it. Every team in the world, every player in the world has experienced it. When my mother sees that I'm a bit down and I complain that things aren't going well, she reminds me: "Try to be positive, that's where it all starts."

Overcoming difficulties

In football, you have to learn that adversity is always on the horizon; you can't simply wish it away. The earlier you face it, the better for you. Not everything is going to go your way.

Early in my career, up to the time I arrived at Valencia, everything seemed to be going according to plan; I was playing and enjoying it. But that was the exception, not the rule.

There are many players who have had to deal with major setbacks early in their careers, but have gone on to reap the rewards later . . .

Just to name a few, I'm going to start with no less a player than Xavi Hernandez, the great Xavi, who unfortunately ruptured the cruciate ligament in one of his knees in 2005. That injury – along with the critics who thought he wasn't good enough to play for Barcelona, that he wasn't vertical enough in his passes, and that he wouldn't fill the space left by Pep Guardiola in FC Barcelona's midfield – created a very tough scenario for Xavi at that time.

What did he do? Firstly, he came back from injury like nothing ever happened, better than before, showing an incredible mental and physical strengh; and then, rather than losing confidence in himself or looking for a move away from Barcelona to escape the critics and comparisons, he came back to play better than ever. (Or, to put it another way, he played as good as always, but came back in a team where his qualities fitted perfectly, where he could shine as he hadn't had a chance to do before).

After that, we know the rest of the story. Trophy after trophy, game after game, he became, without a shadow of a doubt, one of the best and most influential players in the history of Spain and one of the best midfielders in the history of the game. Period.

Of course, no player has ever had an easy path to the top. No one. To name another good friend of Xavi, another majestic player, Andrés Iniesta admitted publicly not so long ago that he suffered from depression in 2009 after winning the treble with FC Barcelona. *Yes, I repeat, after winning the treble with FC Barcelona.*

It can seem to the outside world that you might have it all by winning everything and playing football at the highest level. But being famous can make the mind work in its own way. We are all humans, we all have our personal battles, and nothing, not even recognition or 'success', can stop that.

Andrés, amongst many other examples (Michael Carrick included, as he admitted suffering too), had to go through the experience of facing mental issues and overcoming them. Andrés didn't know was waiting for him. The year after, 2010, he would go and score the goal that would make us, Spain, World Champions. The goal that everyone would want to score, but he did. The most important goal anyone can score. From depression to the top. Nobody deserved it more than him.

Andrés, as Xavi, didn't have it easy and is up there among the most important midfielders in the history of the game. As is Zinedine Zidane, of course. I remember how, at the end of his career, he endured heavy criticism at Real Madrid. If Zidane was criticised, if Messi is criticised, who wouldn't be? Iker Casillas in his last few seasons at Real comes to mind. So does Wayne Rooney. And, of course, Víctor Valdés.

We all agree he was one of the greatest goalkeepers of recent times, but he also received heavy criticism during his time at Barça. Then, just as he was about to join Monaco, a serious knee injury meant the deal was cut short. He literally went from being No1 at Barça (and probably in the world at that time) to 'disappearing' almost completely off the football radar in order to undergo several months of treatment on his own. He did recovery work in Augsburg, in Germany, and took the tram to a public gym every day. He would later say that he remembered how he had to wait for a man to finish using the exercise bike in order to use it himself, just like anyone else in the neighbourhood. He admitted that the experience, although very very difficult, taught him a lot and enabled him to get back in contact with 'real' life, with himself.

No matter how big a player you are, how many things you

have done for a club, nobody escapes criticism, no player avoids difficulties along the way. You have to know that those challenges will arrive. You can't prevent them from affecting you; but how they affect you is something you can work on.

In life, as Victor Frankl once said, 'everything can be taken from a man except one thing: the last of human freedoms – to choose one's attitude in any given set of circumstances, to choose one's own way.' As a footballer, the way in which you react to the challenges you will encounter, will determine your career.

When 'irresponsibility' helps

You would agree with me when I say there are players that don't seem to be nervous before games. They seem like they are going to play football with friends in their backyard, instead of a Premier League game.

Are they actually that relaxed? Is it only a perception from outside? Can you feel like that before an important game? It feels that they simply go out there and play. Easy, right? Not at all.

A friend of mine, the professional handball player Javier Borragán, has told me how he would worry himself sick when some of his team-mates would head out on to the court without seeming to care about the consequences. "I'm playing without confidence, sometimes I don't know how to pass the ball," he would say. "I'm just blocked."

One day I asked him the same question that I've just asked myself (and you): "Do you really think there are people who don't feel any tension before a game and who play better as a result?" "I do," he admitted. "I have team-mates who don't seem bothered about anything at all. They just play and don't fear making mistakes or anything else; they just seem to not care about anything else other than the actual fact of playing itself."

It sounds like the ideal mental state to face a game, right? It is not easy to achieve, of course. Not easy at all.

Mental coaches say that a way of dealing with pre-game nerves is to arrive at the ground knowing that you have done everything you could possibly have done during the week to prepare for the match; then, you will feel more confident when confidence is needed. It surely might be a good way of training your mind towards the competition, as any player would admit that any input is most welcome if it helps to 'perform better'.

Feeling overwhelmed

As a result of the whole mix of mental demands that professionalism can bring to a player's mind, there have been cases where a player can feel paralysed by it, and understandably so. Something of this kind happened to Jesús Navas at the beginning of his career. He didn't exactly feel intimidated on the pitch, but he struggled with feelings of loneliness and anxiety during international call-ups, which stopped him from being selected for the national team until we went to South Africa for the World Cup where he (thankfully given the outcome of the tournament) joined us.

He had being suffering from anxiety whenever he spent long periods of time away from his family and had to look for some help in that matter. With the full support of his club, Sevilla, he overcame the situation and felt confident enough to join the team just in time to win the 2010 World Cup. His recovery was such that he subsequently decided to move countries and sign for Manchester City.

Another very familiar face for me, Bojan Krkić, is also a player who experienced similar issues in terms of feeling overwhelmed, to the point where he had to withdraw from the Euro 2008 squad to recover from anxiety attacks linked to the whirlwind in which he was caught after bursting on to the scene at just 17 years of age.

Too many things were happening too fast and probably too early for him, and that is difficult to handle. He kept it secret at the time, because he was also too young to deal with the media hype that the situation would have generated, but thankfully he also overcame the challenge and went on to have a career filled with experiences in different countries and clubs, scoring lots of goals. Those two are examples of positive reactions after difficult challenges. Both players felt overwhelmed at some point, but they battled through it and came out as stronger players. I am sure of that.

Training the mind from the beginning

Footballers' mental health remains a taboo subject. That's a fact. Although we are seeing more cases being openly admitted by players and managers, much more is known about players' physical conditions, with injuries on display to everyone. That creates the tendency to think that our heads are somehow bomb-proof when in reality, if you think about it, we face a cocktail of ingredients that is prone to bringing on mental health problems.

Many prefer to hide them from the dressing room to

(wrongly) avoid showing some weakness, and that may also go for the people immediately around them. The level of demands still clouds our ability to hold our hands up and admit that we might have a problem, but again, it is a convenient time to remind everyone that players are not machines.

The psychological weight can feel so heavy for some that their performances suffer to such an extent that, on match day, you 'don't recognise' the player who had been so good in training the day before. There are many cases of players who are exceptional in training and look so average in games. How can that be? Again, the mind is knocking at the door.

That's why, in my view, the learning process of mental preparation for the game must start at youth level.

I remember how, at Real Madrid, we had a psychologist called Chema Buceta who would talk to us in groups and help us understand the mental challenges that awaited us in the future.

It's important to coach youngsters on technique and tactics, but it's also vital to prepare them mentally for what lies ahead. I'll give an example of how this could be done.

At Manchester United, one of the mentors for the Under-18s asked his players to build a table using scissors, paper and glue. The players, grouped in teams, did so. Every table, as is normal, had four legs. He then asked them: "Why four legs? why not just one?"

All agreed that four legs would make it more stable. He then asked them to think of themselves as one of these tables. If they only had one leg to stand on – football – what would happen to them if they didn't make it as professional footballers? The mental part of that table, the mental part of the game, should be as important, if not more, than the rest of the components of football, and it should be considered like that from the beginning. I still feel that there is room for improvement in the youth football structure around the world, both for the ones that will make it professionally, and for those who won't.

Flow

It's not surprising that players who are caught in uncertain situations – such as when their future at club level is in doubt or their place in the national team is at risk, but also when they are going through a difficult period in their personal lives – are more likely to pick up injuries.

It seems obvious that, subconsciously, their nervous system is unsettled, their muscles don't react as they should, their bodies feel uncomfortable and their minds end up generating stress that, in extreme cases, can cause real damage.

Even if we like to think that we are not affected by those kinds of situations, I can see why some managers make decisions based on that. For example, for some, Louis van Gaal made a sensible decision when he left David de Gea on the bench when there was speculation about a possible transfer to Real Madrid; and perhaps David did understand, too. It's a time when we tend to feel we are completely fit to play, but it is just impossible. Once David's future was resolved, and I'm sure you all remember the story, he returned to the starting line-up and he swiftly got back to his best, as he always does.

On the other side, when your mind is clear and relaxed, everything seems to flow on the pitch, and I can assure you that this is one the best feelings a player can have. I vividly remember that it happened to me during that – very special – game against Liverpool at Anfield in March 2015, in which I scored two goals.

Strange as it may sound, I felt like the fastest, tallest and strongest player that day. From the beginning, everything felt good, just right. Everything I tried came off: my first control, my first pass, my first shot – when I scored from an Ander Herrera pass.

It felt like I would never lose the ball, like I could beat any player. It felt amazing, I wanted the game to last forever. I wanted to stop time. When I say that the 'flow' state is the best feeling that a player can have during a game, I say that because – based on the theory of the great Mihaly Csíkszentmihaly – being in 'the zone' means 'being in complete absorption in what one does, resulting in loss of one's sense of space and time. It is the mental state of operation in which a person performing an activity is fully immersed in a feeling of energized focus, full involvement, and enjoyment in the process of the activity.' Exactly how I felt that day.

I wouldn't change any single word of that description. What an amazing feeling, right? I am sure you have felt it also at some point in your life, probably more often when you were a kid. Why is it so difficult to maintain that feeling when we grow? If you read Mihaly's magnificent book called 'Flow' you will find the answer.

But like William Bruce Cameron once said, not everything that can be counted counts, and not everything that counts can be counted, so if you ask me why I played so well that day, I'll have no answer.

There was no obvious reason behind it; it wasn't as if anything special had happened to me that week. I just felt good, and although probably subconsciously everything was right in my mind at that time, I have no further explanation. Even worse, the game was an early one, 12:30pm, normally too early for me as you know, but not that time. The pitch was in great condition, it was a beautiful day with the sun beating down, and I felt physically fit. I just remember that I couldn't wait to start the game.

Working on your mind certainly helps boost the performance level, and there are a number of ways to do that. For some, breathing and stretching exercises work well. At Chelsea I used to do yoga, which helped me considerably. Such a routine used to relax me, focused my mind during stressful and pressure-filled situations – and improved my flexibility.

Others try mindfulness. I tried that too and found it very helpful. I've read books about the matter, too, describing techniques to enhance concentration in the present, in your own thoughts and feelings, and on being aware of the world around you. I was very interested in the example of Phil Jackson, the successful coach of the Chicago Bulls and the Lakers, who resorted to mindfulness to clear his players' heads. He was a true pioneer because he managed to get his players to be receptive to something that had previously been completely alien to them and that really helped them.

For others, sometimes, opening up to someone such as a mental coach, letting it all out, taking a weight off the shoulders, helps as well. Listening to music, which has always been part of my pre- and post-match routine, is something that we all do to get the energy going or to release it. At the end of the day, we all need different things, and I consider it very valid to try and do whatever suits you.

Routines and the nonsense

Over my career, I have developed routines for switching off before and after a match that I follow religiously without fail. I don't know why, but doing them makes me feel more ready for the game. I guess we all have them.

I always have a pre-match shower in the hotel before going to the stadium, I always put on first my left shin pad and boot, I always step out on the pitch with my right foot first (just watch me next game) . . .

They are little 'silly' details that have been with me many, many years. I don't really know why I do them, it just feels right. Although I have my little things, yes, some players can be obsessive when it comes to routines before games, carrying out superstitious rituals which can look really crazy from the outside.

I've had team-mates who had to wear a wristband on their left arm because if they didn't, they felt they wouldn't play well. Others wear clothes or socks to death if they believe it brings them luck. David de Gea does it to a T.

He has worn the same shoes with the official Manchester United suit since his first year here, without being bothered that parts of them have visibly worn away. He always orders a ham and cheese omelette for his pre-game meal, without fail. Before every game, he always has a coffee while receiving a massage from the same masseur (Andy). He always sits in the fourth chair of the front row in the meetings until the point that, if someone is sitting in that chair before he arrives, he tells them that we would lose if they don't change the seat with him. They say that goalkeepers are special, and I can confirm that's true with David. I could go on and on . . .

Alexis Ruano, a former team-mate at Valencia, always had to walk between the physios' treatment tables before games, even if it meant taking a detour. He was convinced that he wouldn't play well if he didn't. Yes, I know it is crazy. Sounds like a nonsense. Ángel Di María always wore a necklace and had a medallion of the Virgin in his washbag.

And if we look into different sports, Rafa Nadal is another sportsman with obsessive routines in games, such as not standing on the court markings, touching his sock before heading out, the order in which he drinks his two bottles . . .

Such patterns help you get into the game, but probably at a risk. If and when, one day, they fail you for any reason, or you just forget to do them (which seems difficult to be honest), will you head out on to the pitch with less confidence?

What would Nadal do if that second bottle of water went missing? (He would still probably win anyway, of course). What if David couldn't find his worn-out shoes before going to a game? And what if I step out with the left foot instead of the right? Surely nothing would happen, I know, but while the effort required to do these things is not great, and as nonsensical as it might be, why not do them if they make us feel 'better'?

Imagining the game

Other routines can be suggested by someone else – like the manager. Louis van Gaal always asked us to 'imagine the game' in our hotel room while resting before the matches, and it was something that I've always put into practice.

I do just that without looking for it, subconsciously, in the days prior to every game; I imagine a positive scenario, whether that means visualizing a great piece of play, a goal, a nice assist . . . I don't really know if that helps me or not, as most of the time there is a gap between what you have imagined and what actually happens (unless you are called Messi), but my mind is just so used to doing it.

After playing, especially if the game has been played late in the afternoon or evening, I always struggle to sleep, win or lose, because of the adrenaline which is still flowing through my body.

Most of the time, I remember very vividly in my mind many moments of the games: *that pass that I've missed, that good control I did, that wrong decision I took* . . . it is very difficult for my mind not to go through all of it, whether good or bad actions. I play the game again in my head, only against the pillow this time.

Time to reflect

In football, you have the feeling that everything happens too quickly. Your career simply flies by. You just don't have time to pause everything and think about what you've experienced. The fast-paced rhythm is exhausting.

There are games every few days and you set yourself new targets both weekly, monthly and annually. You get to play under different managers and with different players. It never stops. Your head is focused on the short term and it's hard to take a step back and reflect.

Any player who retires and sits down to think about it will reach the conclusion that his/her career has effectively slipped through his fingers without him or her realising. That's why I think it's so important to savour every season and treat it as something unique.

I remember how, once, during the warm-up for a derby against Manchester City at Old Trafford, it suddenly struck me how our reality was almost surreal. We Manchester United players had got used to a kind of normality which, seen with perspective, was simply extraordinary. I discussed it with Ander Herrera and Marcos Rojo.

"It's unbelievable. When we were kids, could you imagine that we would be here at Old Trafford, where all those greats have played? And now we are here warming up?"

"It's true. I used to watch Manchester United in Argentina when Veron played here and it felt so, so far away, almost impossible to play here. Being here is just crazy," admitted Marcos. Our minds were taking a break to feel the moment, to enjoy the present, to be mindful.

He is right, it is actually crazy.

BUSINESS CLASS

'The importance of money in professional football is indisputable, but it is not important enough to make the game itself secondary' – Jorge Valdano

Nowadays, things have changed. Football players' commitments are many more than just what happens on the pitch. Off the pitch, and especially if you play for a massive club, you will surely have some other duties to perform.

Manchester United, in that respect, brought me closer to understanding the true commercial magnitude of football. Every month, every player has to fulfil activities for our sponsors all over the world. We have featured in adverts in countries such as Thailand, Indonesia, Japan, China, Cameroon and South Africa (just to name a few), as well as film commercials for the United States, Canada, South American countries and the rest of Europe. Some of them recorded in their native language. Yes, you can imagine the laughter . . .

Every shoot was prepared with amazing care, and I realised that Manchester United's influence in the global market is something almost all other teams can only dream of. The club has many employees based in London alone, tasked with seeking out commercial opportunities, and also has offices around the world. One way or another, the club is everywhere. In that sense, it really is an example for other clubs.

This is a side of a professional footballer's life that not all players might enjoy; but, to be honest, it does not bother me that much. I've tried to gain a deeper understanding of how the club's marketing department works – such as when we film advertisements. I jump at the chance to speak to industry professionals and ask them about the art of closing sponsorship deals and how many people work on such and such a task and the type of commercial contracts they are able to bring in.

That's how, thanks to them, I understood how brands were split into different levels, with the Adidas, Chevrolet, AON and Kohler contracts constituting the top of the pyramid structure and other different sectors making up the picture. Every possible gap in the market is taken care of with various brands, all part of a well-defined global strategy. Bringing a brand like Chevrolet on board was key for the US market, while the former agreement with beer company Singha, for example, expanded the club's presence in Asia.

It's always said that Manchester United, as a brand, is a money-making machine and the club's commercial reach certainly confirmed that. None of my previous employers had been able to generate so many shirt sales or secure so many contracts with major brands. But one key thing needs to be remembered. Our club wouldn't have the same impact in the market and value as a brand if it forgot about what made it in the first place: our history, our victories, our football. Authenticity cannot be bought.

To me, growing globally (because if you don't, you probably will not be able to compete with other clubs that do), in amazing fashion, and without sacrificing the identity, while keeping football as the true core of a club, is the only way you create the needed balance between industry and sport. Manchester United has won a lot throughout the generations, and, of course, it's easier to side with the winners rather than the losers. The club is acutely aware of the role its history and its legends have played in its development – proof of which is the fact that Sir Bobby Charlton and Sir Alex Ferguson, two men who have done so much here, are a permanent fixture at Old Trafford. Two great names like these give the club a special, almost unique aura. Obviously, other names, like Giggs, Scholes and Eric Cantona, amongst others, who achieved so much here, also played a big part in building what Manchester United is today.

Personally, it was a pleasure to get to know all of them, as team-mates, managers or partners in Common Goal (as was the case with King Eric). I know he may seem to project a rather peculiar personality from the outside, but everyone who played with him claims that he was a wonderful team-mate, the opposite of an egotist on the pitch. In fact, I've only heard great things about him.

Eric Cantona's son Raphaël has told me that, in his father's day, football was different. Obviously winning was the ultimate goal, but playing entertaining and attractive football, rather than just picking up good results, was also mandatory. He told me how that team, in which those three greats played together, displayed fantastic camaraderie.

The atmosphere was great (it normally is when you keep winning), many players were good friends and would take their children (Raphaël being one of them, Kasper Schmeichel another) with them to the training ground. On top of that, the club lifted the league title practically every year.

I sometimes think that I would have enjoyed playing in a different era, when football was less affected by external interest, by the importance of the business side, and by the winning at all costs mantra. Everything seemed more genuine in the past, and everything seems to be losing its essence in football now. If that makes me a 'romantic', as some call it, then so be it.

Passion

I do understand the sentiment of the many fans who feel that the business side has taken over and that the sport, generally, has lost its authenticity. They even created the concept of opposing what they call 'modern football'. They don't want to be part of a new reality in which agents seem to be more important than fans and have so much influence over teams.

I, too, feel uncomfortable about the way the business side has infiltrated football in many cases. What I like most is the sport itself: training, playing and competing. The rest . . . not so much.

That said, we have to look at both sides. The influx of huge sums of money can lead to greed, selfishness, unfairness and dishonesty in a bid to obtain even more money. But there's a flipside to this negative perception. We also have to think about the number of jobs created in and around the sport, and the amount of people making a life out of it. And that's great.

There is one unquestionable reason behind this incredible financial power that football has: passion. The passion of the millions of believers who not only suffer with defeats, but also spend their money (buying shirts, paying for season tickets, subscribing to TV channels to watch games . . .) for their team. And in order to respect them and to respect football as we know it, they should never be forgotten.

Salaries

There is also the perception, and it's a reality comparing football players with 99 per cent of society, that players earn a lot. Many people cannot comprehend when a player earning £3million a year demands a raise. But, for me, there is a deeper conversation here.

Players don't set the rates. If we are in a world in which football operates with such amounts of money, should it not be players, the main actors of the show, who get the bigger part? I think so.

Please, don't get me wrong. I am not saying that football players' wages are not obscene, they are, but given the situation in which we live, with professional football as it is, football players' wages are far more 'deserved' than the wages of many other figures in our industry.

When it comes to wage demands and contract negotiations, we obviously compare ourselves with our team-mates and players at other clubs at our levels, and again, I think that's normal in any sector. If a journalist negotiates a new deal, they won't ask for the same wage as an architect or a plumber. You compare yourself with others in your trade.

I've also been asked if I'm embarrassed to earn so much money. I don't think that embarrassed is the right word. Shocked, probably is more accurate. Thinking about it, there's no reason to be embarrassed for earning something that you don't earn illegally. I simply play a sport and receive a salary for doing so. Sport has become a 'bubble' and salaries are part of that bubble, yes, but it's not like the corrupt politician who steals money from society and uses it for their own benefit. *That* is embarrasing.

And talking about that bubble, I recognise that I live a different reality than, for example, my friends. We could say that 'real' or 'usual' life is what they, who had to study and earn a living somewhere in Spain or abroad have experienced. Just like members of my family, they have had to deal at times with unemployment and very tough periods. That's what 99 per cent of people go through.

There is often talk about how players, because they earn so much money, become 'idiots' who believe they have inde-structible powers. Well, I disagree. I think that if you are an idiot, you are one even before you get money, and the only thing that money does is multiply it.

Of course, money can certainly help you lead a more

comfortable life, travel, maybe solve some health problems, etc . . . but I've never been madly obsessed with money. I guess it might be because since a very early age, I was earning good amounts, and never had to experience what most people do. If my life had been different, maybe I would not be able to say the same.

If you think about it, the truth is that we are not ready for the amount of money that we earn. It is simply impossible to be mature enough, in your 20s, to be able to cope with it with ease. Youth, fame, money – the perfect mix to lose your mind. There are many well-known cases of sportsmen who earned millions and millions in five or 10 years, only to throw it all away in a year or less. That's why it's important to raise awareness among people with careers like ours, so that they spend their dosh responsibly in order to preserve their financial future.

I signed my first professional contract with Real Madrid Castilla at 18, for an annual salary of €90,000. Of course, that was a huge sum of money for someone of my age and the figures have continually increased over time. Back then, my parents decided that I needed to ask financial advisors to help me. What a great decision that was. Although you earn a lot, you also take on huge responsibility because no matter how young you are, you know that a player's career is very short and you better put a solid financial structure in place to build a safe future for you and your family.

Image

Another aspect of modern day football is the ever-growing presence of sponsorship deals that tend to come along with those first few contracts. Again, especially in the beginning of our careers, we are in a situation that we have to make decisions without being really ready for them.

Some players try to get as many brands on board as possible and squeeze as much money as they can out of their image. And I can understand the logic given the short duration of a player's career, but, ultimately, I started to see it differently.

During my first steps in professional football I made some decisions that I would not repeat if I had to make them today, and most of them are related to sponsorships. Fortunately, I changed my mindset and now I always try to ensure that each proposal I get involved with fits with my personality so it makes it genuinely more meaningful.

If you ask me the best example of a sports personality in terms of his/her image and reputation, one name instinctively comes to my mind: Roger Federer. As a top tennis star, he is associated with major brands that fit with his image as a respected and admired human being who is a genuine sportsman. All his sponsors are an extension of his tennis style, the best in their sectors. They represent what he represents – to me, elegance and excellence.

On the other hand, there are many cases of top athletes associated with brands that have nothing in common with how they are as people or what they represent. You only need to put on the TV for a few minutes to realise that.

The hidden army

Support at football clubs comes from an army of workers whose names are unknown outside the club, and who are also a key part of the industry. You won't see them in the foreground, but that doesn't mean they don't make a significant contribution to their club. This business doesn't just depend on the people heading up footballing projects: the owners, chairmen, directors and managers. Take away these other employees and what would work?

One of the good things about football is the personal connections you make with club employees on the back of spending so many hours together at the training ground. We footballers spend a lot of time in our own world. We train, we play and we train again. Rewind, repeat. But behind closed doors, almost everything is done for us, starting in pre-season.

You have transport arranged for everything, whether it's going to hotels, training or stadiums. You have problems at home? There are club employees (the 'player care department') who are there to help at the other end of the phone, even if it's just to help pay the electricity bill. It's ideal in terms of players spending as much time as possible focusing on their physical and mental preparation – provided you've got the right kind of personality to be cared for like that.

But there is a risk too. There will come a time after retirement when the player will have to pay the bills him or herself, and won't know how to do it. When the bubble bursts, you have to fend for yourself. If you don't, you'll find yourself cut off from life.

Roles within the club range from coaches, physios, kit men, rehabilitation coaches, the medical department and the media team to the kitchen staff – such as chef Michael Donnelly and his assistant Jofre. Then you have the security staff who lift the barrier at the training ground and travel with us for games; swimming pool staff; groundsmen and receptionists such as Kath – who, you may remember, has been at the club for almost 50 years and outlasted even Sir Alex Ferguson.

Inevitably, you end up forging friendships with many of them. It's a far cry from the cold image that people may have of footballers or of the industry as a whole. We all depend on one another.

Of course we are the players, but they're the ones who get our kits ready, look after us when we're in pain and boost us with a quick chat that may help us forget about a bad performance. Their contribution should be acknowledged when explaining the reasons why a club has won trophies.

They are fundamental to creating the chemistry that you need to achieve success. They are lovely, normal people who help you perform and, in turn, you feel very pleased for them when the team enjoys success. And, really important, you end up really missing them whenever you change clubs.

Football and the city

For all the criticism directed at the concept of the football 'industry', Manchester is a clear example of a metropolis that has benefited hugely from being home to two big football clubs. If you speak about Manchester in any corner of the globe, the first thought that runs through people's heads is football, alongside music, given the city's tradition of famous bands. Then, maybe, some people will think about its historic role in the Industrial Revolution. But the first thought is football.

Having a club of Manchester United's size has enhanced the city's reputation way beyond British borders. Even people who follow the Premier League would be far likelier to know how to locate Manchester on a map than those who don't follow football.

Here is a fact: Old Trafford is the city's biggest tourist attraction. The stadium tours start every seven or eight minutes all day long, almost every day of the year, and they are packed. Hotels near the ground are always fully booked on matchdays, with the hotel trade, restaurants, taxis and many other sectors cashing in on the tens of thousands of people passing through. I remember when, after a game, I had to head straight to the airport to join the national team, and the terminal was packed with United shirts. I didn't know how many people actually travelled to watch our games from abroad. Incredible.

As players, we are perfectly aware that we are in a privileged situation and in a position to help many people by doing something that we enjoy, which is playing football. We can reach so many of them, motivate them and create excitement by doing that alone.

I often receive letters from fans who have been admitted to hospital with a serious illness who have told me the only thing that they enjoyed was following Manchester United matches and watching me score.

We are so privileged to have the power to bring so many people together through football. It doesn't matter if they are left or right-wing, rich or poor, when their team scores a goal, they hug whoever is by their side without knowing who they are or what they own.

Music and football are the only two global industries capable of generating such reactions, in stark contrast with politics which has been more divisive than ever recently. That power isn't being maximised at present, but there's still plenty of scope to direct it through a series of initiatives that improve people's lives, and I fully intend to 'do my bit'.

Sport is a fundamental tool for improving society's well-being in developed and under-developed countries. Football promotes good habits from a young age and can also help reduce social problems. If you train in a neighbourhood where living conditions are precarious, football is a healthy distraction that can help youngsters stay out of trouble and keep them on the right path. Playing the game should be a guaranteed right for all children.

I've collaborated with UNICEF, Laureus, Aldeas Infantiles, Cáritas and Save the Children, but an organisation that mainly used football as a tool to try to improve the world was missing from that list.

I finally came across a non-governmental organisation (NGO) that combined my passion for the game with charitable causes when StreetFootballWorld got in touch with me. They had been active for 15 or 20 years by that point, but had never resorted to advertising until they felt it was time to find some ambassadors who could spread the word about their work. They've been growing a network of around 150 local organisations all over the world, under the StreetFootballWorld umbrella, that receive targeted aid to build facilities and pitches for children and use football as a means of improving their lives.

It isn't just operating in Third World countries, but also in Europe and North America. Other initiatives include solidarity tourism trips from the First World to the Third

World. They promote trips for students in the USA, who are about to start at university. They have the chance to pay for a unique experience in Africa, where they can mix with local people and play football together. The money contributes to improving living conditions in those communities.

Football is a power for good

Aside from being a business, football must also embrace its duty to help society. And the reality is that football is also involved in community and charity work like no other industry. I think it's unfair when players' or clubs' participation in charitable events is thought of as nothing but an attempt to clean up their image. No. Wrong. And besides, let's potentially accept that it might be for image: so what? The important thing is to act, *to do it,* which is far more accountable than people who speak a lot but do nothing.

In that sense, the United Kingdom has set the benchmark in the field with its charitable traditions, which go back to the earliest stages of football in the country. Charities are an intrinsic part of this country's social structure and football is no stranger to charitable giving. Every single Premier League club organises charitable activities and offers services to the community through their foundations, with players performing an active role throughout.

In many cases the help is targeted in the local area because, as the saying goes, charity starts at home, rather than an anonymous donation to somebody thousands of miles away.

The MU Foundation collaborates with around 200 schools in the area. I think it's brilliant that both the Premier League and the FA are so committed to running social welfare programmes and ensure clubs make such a positive contribution to their surrounding areas. Another example is the fact that gate receipts from the Community Shield go to charity, further evidence that English football's social structure has a lot going for it.

To speak about something close to me, the MU Foundation holds 'Dream Days' a few times a year, when children with terminal illnesses come to the training ground and get the chance to meet their idols. It's always absolutely heartbreaking to be told the news that one of the children has passed away a few months later.

I particularly remember a five or six-year-old boy who came to the dressing room with his father after a match against Bournemouth. He had a Manchester United shirt, which we all signed. A few minutes later I noticed that his father hadn't uttered a word and was taking a back seat throughout. He was silently crying because he knew that his son was fulfilling a dream and only had two months left to live. The boy was completely unaware that he didn't have long left. On the contrary, he smiled throughout, absolutely thrilled, as if he didn't have a care in the world. You don't forget things like this. How could you?

Whenever we visit children in hospital over Christmas time, we see youngsters in total agony who don't want visitors and sometimes may not even realise that Manchester United players have come to see them, until that moment when they open their eyes and a small smile breaks out on their faces. Their parents are often in tears and thank us for generating that small moment of happiness in such an extreme situation. The power of football really is invaluable.

I must accept that such experiences are a reality check. I find it tough and notice myself struggling when I leave, but it's also a reminder of how lucky we are to be healthy. It puts any sad day that I may have after losing a game into perspective.

Like many others, when I'm asked to take part in such initiatives, I don't check to see if there are too many of them or not. Why would you stop helping because you've previously been involved in other charitable activities? In my point of view, they are certainly not mutually exclusive. You should be known as *Mister Yes* in that sense.

When winning is all

I am sorry to say that I am not a blind optimist when it comes to the future of the game on the pitch, despite what you've just read may suggest.

I have my doubts too, particularly when it comes to the game itself, to what happens on the pitch, and one aspect of it in particular: the importance which is now given to the result, as if winning really was, not the main thing, but the 'only' thing.

That 'only' is crucial. The process no longer matters; it's only the effect of the process that matters. The actual show, the beauty, is not the priority.

I'm afraid to see football becoming less and less about beauty. Why? Because results decide manager's futures, and the fear of losing becomes more important than the bravery you need to show to go for a win.

Quite naturally, there are still few people who don't seem to be afraid of being sacked. In football management, there's Marcelo Bielsa, but there aren't many Bielsas in the world.

That focus put only on the end product is creating gradually less attacking football, tighter football, in which 'artists' or creative players per se no longer have a place. Which top club would buy a Valeron these days? Or a Riquelme? 'Too slow,' they'd say.

So, as you can see, I have my reservations about the future of the game.

But while there's plenty of talk about the football industry and the negative connotations linked to it, I prefer to focus on the game's power as the most beautiful and engaging sport in the world.

As long as football keeps the essence of the game and remains a catalyst for emotions that ring true, I'd rather see that business, and all the things that brings with it, in positive terms overall.

20

EGO TRIP

'To be able to deal with different personalities is probably more important than any tactics' – Zinedine Zidane

As you know, the experience of my first year at Valencia and what I gained from it, made a deep impression on me. I'd even go as far as saying that it helped me greatly to be who I am, as a footballer, and as a man, too. There were so many tests – none of which I had really seen coming and was prepared for – in a single season, which forced me to come on leaps and bounds as a professional at just 19 years of age. Too much, too early.

Jumping some years ahead, I've encountered some team-mates that had to face similar circumstances. Marcus Rashford was one of them. I remember how he came into the dressing room as an extremely shy person, exactly what you would expect for a kid of his age (unless you are called Zlatan Ibrahimovic).

But Marcus integrated himself into the squad, especially

in the beginning, thanks to his great qualities as a player, performances and goals, rather than his words. It was a similar story for Anthony Martial, another reserved character who truly comes to life on the pitch and who scored against Liverpool on his debut. The best possible introduction. Both of them, just like I did at Valencia, developed quick under tough circumstances (not good enough results, managers being sacked . . .).

I have to say here that I have special predilection for Anthony Martial. For me, he is one of those players that can win a game by themselves. A superior player. From our first training session together, you could see the way he plays, taking people on and enjoying himself. The only thing you have to do when you play with him is give him the ball back where he wants it and he will do the rest. I love this kind of player.

Off the pitch it's another story, his personality is just different; introverted, shy. But I like that too. I like the type of player who does his talking on the pitch. Many players come to my mind who express themselves freely and confidently with a ball at their feet and who don't feel as outgoing off it, such as Andrés Iniesta and Lionel Messi.

What happens on the pitch, stays on the pitch

So that's exactly how I overcame those hurdles at Valencia myself, gradually adapting thanks to the fact that all was going well in football terms for me. As my importance on the pitch grew, so did my confidence within the squad, and my understanding of what it meant to be part of it.

As is the case at any workplace, you quickly realise that you aren't automatically a group of 25 best friends, rather you may have three or four, the rest being team-mates, which is fine.

You know that the manager's decisions can affect personal relationships (although they shouldn't). All 25 have the same objective, which is to play. And if two of us compete for the same position, one will get the nod, while the other will be left out, and that is that, just how it should be.

While I quickly understood that there was no need for everybody to become best friends with each other, I also understood that if a relationship isn't the greatest off the pitch, it doesn't necessarily have to have a negative influence on what happens on it.

I didn't see a single case of a poor relationship being transferred on to the playing field. Yes, there were a few cases of problems between players at Valencia, but you'd never have guessed that when they were together on the field. We were all professionals, we knew that we had to run for each and every one of our team-mates, and that we would all suffer the consequences if we didn't respect that fundamental rule. We didn't compromise the common good for personal problems.

What is interesting and I assume would not surprise you is that it works another way as well. Positive connections are often translated into the game. To give you an example, it was obvious that I have a great friendship with Ander Herrera and we understood football the same way, so a quick glance between us would be enough to know what the other was about to do, almost every single time. Other examples that spring to mind are Messi and Suarez or Messi and Alves, or perhaps, some years ago, Torres and Gerrard.

Sometimes it feels like you will find each other with closed eyes on the pitch, and that, of course, benefits the team.

'There is no need to turn off the other's light in order to make ours shine' – Gandhi

I've always tried to be as generous to my team-mates as I could and to put the lid on any envy or jealousy I may feel. But I'm no saint. Inevitably, the ego creeps through at times, as when my desire to play and my frustration at not being able to has got the better of me. Like everybody else in this world, I've said to myself sometimes: *I don't understand why I'm not playing and so-and-so is. I can give more than him, I am a better player than him.*

I might have been right, or not, whatever, but what I quickly learnt was how to prevent that negativity from affecting my behaviour towards others. I don't believe in succeeding by treading on others anyway. I genuinely feel that, deep down, I'm a fighter. But my way of fighting – for my place in the team, in this case – has always been by trying to make my qualities stand out, rather than focusing on the negatives of others.

It might also be a matter of pride: I prefer to play when I've really earned my place in the manager's eyes, rather than when I replace an underperforming team-mate or because of injuries. What is more, I've always been fearful of wishing bad on others for my own benefit. I believe it's something that will always end up coming back to haunt me. Karma, if you like.

So I thought it was a better and more useful reaction to put myself in the other person's shoes, which, in this particular instance, means looking at how a team-mate who isn't playing much can keep training hard, no matter what his feelings may be, as was the case with Paulo Ferreira at Chelsea, or Lee Grant at United. Two examples of magnificent and impeccable professionals that gave their best even knowing that they would not play week after week. With players like them, everybody's a winner in the end, especially the team.

A team in which there is zero empathy between players is not a good team in the purest sense.

'More the knowledge, lesser the ego; lesser the knowledge, more the ego' – Albert Einstein

You can believe in yourself, in your talent, in your merit, but you can do all that without making a show of it. That for me is the beauty of humility.

One of the best players in the history of the game lives by it. A master, a genius, and as humble a man that has ever kicked a football. I even heard him say one day: "Bloody hell, if I'd known about all the fuss, maybe I shouldn't have scored that goal!"

Those words came out of Andrés Iniesta's mouth during a national team visit to a military base. We had just lifted the trophy in South Africa, but World Cup fever kept burning at home for some time. The whole squad was there, but, obviously, the soldiers cheered Andrés passionately as soon as he came through the door. They would end up chanting his name. Of course, that was not the only occasion; they did that everywhere we went.

Anyone else in his shoes would have felt on top of the world after scoring the winning goal in the final against the

Netherlands and knowing what this meant for the rest of his career and his public image, but in some ways it felt like it was too much for Andrés. He just wasn't comfortable with all the fuss that he created. The comment he made at the military base was mainly in jest, yes, but deep down it showed that he didn't feel at ease in his role, he didn't need all that public recognition to fulfill his ego in a way. Normality and humility plus greatness, that's Andrés' formula.

Of course, throughout my career I've shared dressing rooms with some other players without an ounce of what people call 'ego' running through their bodies. Players like (just to name a few) Carlos Marchena, Santi Cazorla, Adrián López, Petr Čech, Matteo Darmian, Aritz Aduriz, Xavi Hernández, Sergio Busquets and Oriol Romeu, who is, without a doubt in my mind, the clearest example of how modesty can be the quality of a successful professional sportsman.

Ori is the best. He has a huge heart, and I still remember how he made his home in London a 'safe house', so that friends of his who hadn't got a job could go there and earn a living by doing shift work at restaurants or clothes shops. His personality, kindness and professionalism are sadly not very common in the football world nowadays.

Just as there are players who stand out on the pitch, but who find it remarkably easy to keep living 'normal', even 'conventional' lives as seen from the outside, there are other professionals who need to be constantly in the limelight to motivate themselves, which, in some ways, is a logical reaction.

Every player in the world, myself included, likes to feel important. It also happens to an employee in a company who will head into work in better spirits every day if they feel valued. But that deep desire to feel important shouldn't be confused with having a big ego.

Experts on that matter say that when someone always needs to be the centre of attention, that person is showing a lack of confidence in certain parts of their personality. A kind of weakness. And that's exactly how ego can affect you, the bigger your ego is, the weaker you might be deep inside you.

Society of ego

There's nothing quite like social media networks for understanding just how this process works. In the era of 'likes', 'follows' and 'look at how good my life is' versus the reality, ego plays a key role.

The need for attention, for followers, for recognition is developing beyond sanity. And, of course, it has reached the football world, how could it not?

After training, it's common to see many players (me included, although I am trying to change that pattern), jump straight on to their mobiles to check who has written on WhatsApp, what new emails you have, or just to open Instagram and check what's happening on there. And I tell you, time stops when your finger keeps scrolling down and suddenly you have been sitting with your training clothes on for 15 minutes without realising. I am sure it happens to you too (perhaps minus the training clothes). It's scary.

We live in an era in which inter-personal communication is in serious decline because of the abuse of new technology. In football, face-to-face relationships continue to prevail, at least during the 90 minutes in which everything depends on our connection as a group: I don't know of a single team that can play football with their mobiles in their hands. Yet.

And, of course, as a football player, you get many mentions, many direct messages, and you subconsciously start checking them too. You check the likes that your last photo has 'earned', you check how many more followers you have and how many other players have . . . and you become a victim of it, that society of ego. I know: it's happened to me. But, thankfully I've realised, probably later than I should, and I try to keep distance more and more from this kind of 'addictive pattern', so common in dressing rooms.

But the 'misuse' of social media isn't just a problem among football players, as you don't just find egos in football changing rooms, of course, but in all areas of our sport (and society). It's a human thing. You also find egotistical executives and owners who are more focused on preserving their reputation than on their company's interests. There are famous journalists who believe that they and only they have the right opinions. There is ego everywhere.

It's harmful to society as a whole when it starts focusing only on the individual, with less willingness to look at the whole picture. Materialistic photos and compulsive selfie-taking have become a very big part of our times. Too many people are worried about presenting a version of their life that isn't necessarily real, and when that happens, in the long term, that 'lie' will end up destroying you.

Remember where you come from

You have to learn by experience, they say, and mine arrived quite early. The first chance to feed that ego of mine arose when my career took off as a teenager. Signing for Real Madrid was a huge deal for me and everyone around me. I then made my La Liga debut for Valencia at 19 and won my first trophy, the Copa del Rey. I made my Spain debut a few months later. It was all happening so, so fast.

At times like these, you're bombarded with praise, and if you're not careful, you can start feeling you're better than the rest. Flattery can have a negative effect on your development at such a key age, when your personality is still forming. Praise can make you lower your guard, but it made me hungrier to reach the top. It's important not to forget where you come from when it all starts to 'happen'; important, even crucial to be aware that those around you, namely friends and family, are key to your success. Everyone needs an anchor.

As you improve by making mistakes, I of course made some too . . . I had that one silly summer during my teenage years where, on one of our summer trips, I seemed to pay more attention to my phone than to my friends. At the time I didn't realise, of course. "It was the only time when you were different, where you didn't seem like yourself. You were on a different planet". *Ouch.* I'm glad it seemed to be just that isolated episode.

From that moment I always try to remind myself of that truth: you must never forget the people around you who have always been there, both in the good times and the bad. You have to be grateful to the people who have helped you get to where you are, because there's never been a great player or a world beater who has done it all on his/her own.

This is not a cliché. It is really down to your team-mates, coaches and the people around you. Forget it, and you forget yourself. They are guidelines that can soothe an ego problem and also be applied to our society, which, sadly, is increasingly dominated by the 'me, me, me' culture.

A story about an autograph

To frame the importance of football in society and to give you one more example of how it can be very easy to let your ego grow, allow me to take you to back to Oviedo, in 2010 this time.

Just months after winning the World Cup, the national team was awarded probably one of the most important awards in Spain, the Premio Príncipe de Asturias of Sports (now Princess of Asturias), a very prestigious ceremony which celebrates professionals the world over who have stood out in various fields.

So there I was, representing the team among other team-mates in front of my family, just yards away from my home, my school, my roots – I remember that very vividly, my family could not be prouder, especially my grandmother. Before taking the stage, as is usual, all the winners were waiting for the event to start in a room next to the auditorium at the Teatro Campoamor in Oviedo. And then it happened. The other award winners, world-famous names in their fields such as author Amin Maalouf and sculptor Richard Serra, amongst the other incredibly talented people that were with us in that room, started to ask for our autographs. *Really?* I thought. *We just play football.*

I mean, to deserve an award like that you must have done something really amazing and unique in your field, and they were asking for our signatures for their grandchildren.

Instantly, my mind realised, once more, the power and reach of our sport. Yes, we made a lot of people happy by winning that tournament, but surely these other winners did things with greater value for society? An award for Communication and Humanities, or International Co-operation, or Technical and Scientific Research should be more admired (or at least the same) as sport if you ask me, so the autograph maybe should have been the other way around, from them to us.

Times change

Given that it's a team sport, it might be natural to assume that football teaches you to be more of a team player and less individualistic. But the higher up in the game you go, the more individualism you can come across. You notice players' egos with greater clarity at the top level; this said, you can also detect the problem at youth level.

There are children who only think about themselves, and whose parental advice is to only think about themselves. How wrong is that? Unbelievable. Also, and driven by the social media obsession I talk about, many kids try to copy their idols by imitating their haircut, their celebrations, and wearing the same boots they wear. Back in my day – here I am, talking like a grandad, when I'm 31 – there wasn't as much noise about trivial matters. What mattered most was scoring goals, not the way you celebrated them. What mattered most was your control, your passes, not the haircuts.

Face to face

Even if the use of smartphones has become big, face-to-face communication (and confrontation) still remains part of the day-to-day life of a dressing room, a mechanism by which we joke around, and can solve problems between us, and which demands very sensitive and determined handling by the manager and the senior players.

We're under added pressure in this sport, with public scrutiny constantly hanging over us that inevitably leads to moments of extreme tension, where players lose their heads and can even come to blows. I've experienced problems of this kind in almost every team that I've been part of, but it's never really amounted to much: usually, a heated moment in training caused by frustration or a misplaced comment made after training or a match that someone didn't like. For me, the face-to-face communication remains the most effective way to interact. The most human, at least, that's for sure.

Seeing red

As for me, I can't remember holding a grudge against a team-mate throughout my career; yes, there has been the odd flashpoint on the training pitch.

For example, managers usually referee small-sided games in training and may not award what you think is a deserved free-kick, just to keep the game flowing, and so you start to get worked up. The next foul isn't given either and by the time the third one happens, you see red and kick your team-mate, only to later think what a complete fool you have been and regret it. I've been tested that way many times, for it is a test.

Managers do it because referees sometimes won't give fouls and so it's a matter of managing that instantaneous burst of rage to ensure you don't get sent off when you're confronted by the real thing.

Making excuses for yourself is pointless. Awareness of your mistake is enough. When I miss a clear-cut chance or a penalty, fluff a pass or miscontrol the ball, it remains etched on my mind and I try to ensure it will not happen again.

A clear example was the first red card of my career, in a game against West Brom. We ended up losing 1-0. I felt that it was harsh, of course I did, but I also knew I could have avoided being shown two silly yellow cards in something like three minutes. I wasn't feeling particularly angry on the pitch; I was simply shocked, as it had never happened to me before. I simply put my foot where I shouldn't have and ended up leaving the team a man down with more than an hour to play. I felt awful. It was my error, and we paid for it on the pitch.

How you react to a mistake which has cost your side dear, and how the rest of the team reacts to it too, is key.

Without labels

The world nowadays seems to be divided into winners and losers, success and failure, rich and poor, and reaching big targets or getting left behind.

I believe that we should make more of life and focus on what really matters instead of always labelling people, instead of always judging. I believe that we should leave our egos aside as much as we can, or at least, not feed them constantly.

21

SECOND CHANCES

'Reinventing oneself is life' – Martin Rius (ALS victim,
a friend of mine and source of motivation)

The career of a football player passes by very quick. Every footballer would tell you the same. It feels like yesterday when I was doing my presentation for Valencia. But suddenly, and without having much time to digest everything that happened over the last 12 years, here I am. Honestly, it goes scarily quick.

I feel that I still want to, and can, play for many years, but I also need to be realistic and know that I will not be playing professional football forever.

Two of my former Manchester United team-mates, with whom I played in my first year at the club, Rio Ferdinand and Anders Lindegaard, opened up my eyes to the need to prepare for that future long before retirement – whatever 'long' means in a football life. Thinking about it now, both of them (good friends with each other) always seemed to have something new in the pipeline.

Rio in particular was never short of a plan or several. At that time, he was already involved in many projects: his magazine, his music label, his clothing brand, his own foundation, his restaurants and his books . . . and now, his punditry.

But Rio, with his gift for communication, his personality and his open-mindedness, was also much more than this. He was, and is, a generous man, which he shows through the work done by his charity, and which he also showed to me, on a different level when I joined Manchester United, by helping me to settle in like few others did or could have done, given his status at the club and within the English game.

Of course, many other players have shown this gift for reinvention too, people like Eric Cantona (prolific actor) and, in a very different style, Gary Lineker; people like David Beckham, the perfect example of a former footballer who has branched out into many different professional spheres and found a way to do the things that he loves on a daily basis.

As for me . . . who knows? As much as I try to think ahead and 'prepare' for what could come, I honestly don't know what I am going to do yet. But what I do know is that football has given me a great privilege: the financial ability to decide what I want to do in the future, and not many people are able to do that, unfortunately.

Do I want to be involved in the sport as a pundit?

I don't know, as I always had my reservations about some former players who become pundits and, whether they realise it or not, end up making many destructive comments and being overly critical, seeming to forget, at times, that they've once played and made mistakes too, of course.

Do I want to become an agent?

Do I want to become a manager or sports director?

Who knows. Maybe I'll end up doing things that have nothing in common with football, although I know it might not take long for me to feel the need to get back on to the pitch and get that matchday feeling back. I remember Ryan Giggs and Vicente del Bosque telling us again and again to enjoy our careers as much as possible, because we will miss them terribly once it is over.

That drug is impossible to flush completely out of the system. I noticed it with Giggs when he was Van Gaal's assistant, or now with Carrick as our assistant coach, from the way they got on the ball whenever they could. You could feel they were desperate to get out there again and put in some more crosses and passes. They would probably have been able to do it better than most, if not all of us, even now. One loses the fitness, but one never loses the touch.

That's why I'm not ruling out staying connected to the football world, of course. I'm fully aware that it will be very tough to distance myself from it, especially when people like Ander Herrera, who is crazy about the sport, often jokes about us being the perfect coaching duo.

But yes, as I said before, I have thought and think about my life 'afterwards'. For us, footballers, it's normal to start to think about retirement once we hit the halfway point of our careers, I would say. It obviously doesn't even cross your mind when you're 21 or 22 and are beginning to show signs that you could grow into a player. At that age, projecting yourself into the future without playing football doesn't make much sense. *What future?* You live in the present, and you squeeze as much out of it as you can, because 'the end' seems so far away. But once you turn 28-ish, the time has come to consider what may come after you hang up your boots in six or seven years' time – if you're lucky (or 12 if you are Ryan Giggs!).

It's time to go 'back to school', get ready for the hereafter. It could be learning a new language, getting your coaching badges, or, in my case, trying to complete my university studies, although I don't know if I'll eventually end up practising marketing or sports science and physical education. But completing my degrees would at least give me the chance to assess two vastly different fields of work when I retire. The alternatives are grim.

Avoiding the pitfalls

Sadly, for many, when that moment arrives, the struggle starts. It is well known that a number of ex-players encountered different kind of problems while playing that were aggravated after retiring, such as Paul Gascoigne, Tony Adams, Mágico González . . .

Retirement can be tough, as contradictory as it sounds. The routine that you've been automatically following since your teenage years, split into training, travelling and playing matches, suddenly comes to a halt; it might be difficult to change and create a new rhythm. You might have the rest of your life ahead of you, but little idea of how to approach it. You go from being a headline-maker to a 'forgotten man' in the blink of an eye, which many people are unable to digest. You go from 100 miles an hour to a standstill in the space of a month – perhaps I should say 'a day', as it is that brutal.

Financial security is not a given either, unless you've listened to the advice of trustworthy advisors. Divorces are common, so are alcohol-related problems and gambling addictions. Here you are, in your mid-30s, old in the football world, but still young in real life. In many ways, it's a fresh start. For others, it's a final stop. The days of being the centre of attention as a footballer are over and, for some, it is a devastating experience. And if you haven't started preparing the ground while you were still playing, there is a good chance you could follow the same path.

Playing to a different beat

To avoid these kind of situations, thankfully, structures have been put in place to help manage this transition. Support is available for players who look to get their coaching badges or want to complete a sports director course, which some FAs allow you to do in an abridged form after taking your time constraints into consideration.

Furthermore, there are organisations, such as the AFE, the Association of Spanish Footballers, in Spain and the PFA in England, which help guide retired players through that potentially traumatic period. There are also football clubs helping their ex-players (every club should do this in my opinion), and groups of former players who have been through that themselves and know exactly what a footballer might need to come through a rough patch. In this respect, things have improved considerably in recent times.

Football to change the world

One thing I know for sure, one of the few things I'm certain of about my future, is that I will always be involved in 'football for good', even after my playing career.

It is undoubtedly one of the closest causes to my heart, and it is a great opportunity to put the platform I enjoy as a player at the service of something I believe in, and which – I hope – will last long after the name 'Mata' has disappeared from a teamsheet. It gives a deeper meaning to what being a professional football player is.

That's why on August 4, 2017, I launched something that I, with the assistance of others within the world of football, hoped would help change the world, even if only in some small way. Something which was born out of my love for football, out of what I'd experienced through it, like that extraordinary, life-changing moment in the Allianz Arena five years before. The Champions League final.

After we scored that equaliser: I just knew. When we went to penalty kicks: I still knew. When Didier Drogba stepped up to take the final penalty, I was sure he was going to score. I think the expression on his face after the ball went in said everything. He didn't know whether to cry or laugh. He was overwhelmed, like we all were. And as soon as the craziness died down — I immediately thought of my family.

Everyone was there in the crowd that night: my dad, mum, grandparents, friends. I knew the penalties must have been stressful for them – especially my poor grandmother. Later on, someone told me that she had been so nervous that she actually had to hide in the bathroom towards the end of the match.

But it was in this exact moment, when we were celebrating, when I looked around at my team-mates, and I saw something truly beautiful, and which football is one of very few things to offer.

We had a keeper from the Czech Republic, a defender from Serbia, and another from Brazil, midfielders from Ghana, Nigeria, Portugal, Spain and England; and, of course, one unique striker from the Côte D'Ivoire. We came from all over the world, our backgrounds had little in common, and we spoke many different languages.

Some had grown up in countries ravaged by war, some had grown up in poverty, others, like me, in peace and relative comfort; but there we were, all standing together in Germany, as the new champions of Europe.

The way we had come together from all around the world to work for a common goal was something that struck me. What about using that unique bond which football can create between strangers to change the world for the better?

Common Goal is born

Without a doubt, one of the most important people in my life, my grandad, was a source of inspiration in every single aspect. Especially in the most difficult moments.

I remember calling him one night when I was struggling, and his words have stayed with me ever since. "Your football and your career, Juan, they give me life. I feel so proud and I am filled with hope when I watch you."

That call had a tremendous impact, not just on me, but also on the way I thought about football. What I was doing in my career wasn't just about me. It was about us. I was playing because I brought joy to people in different ways than just by scoring goals. My grandfather was the living embodiment of this feeling, and after I realised that, I made sure to keep that thought with me at all times.

I also remember another telephone conversation with him – he had still never missed a professional match of mine – which took place when I was a Manchester United player, at a time when he was very sick.

We had beaten Saint-Étienne 1–0 in France in a Europa League match. His voice was weak. I could tell that he was struggling. His words came out slowly, but he told me that my assist to Henrikh Mkhitaryan during that match had been great. That was probably the most special assist of my life because it was the last one my grandfather ever saw. A few days later, he passed away.

You know when something important happens in your life and you remember exactly where you are? I remember everything from that match and the bus ride home. And I hope that when I see my grandfather again we can speak about it.

I flew to Spain to go to his funeral a short time later. When I came back to Manchester and turned on my phone, I saw all the messages from the United supporters on social media – and it meant the world to me.

We won the next match we played, a League Cup final against Southampton. But afterwards, I felt a little, how can I put it? Hollow. I didn't have my grandfather to share the victory with.

One of the things in football, and in life, that I'm most proud of is that I have been able to share my greatest moments with my family; but at that moment, when I desperately wanted to speak with my grandfather, I couldn't. So instead I began to reflect.

I started thinking about everything football had given me. And I thought about what I wanted my legacy to be. I knew how lucky I was to have the opportunities I'd had – and that not everyone has a family like mine. Even though I'd done some work with NGOs before, I knew that I wanted to do something more, something different: I wanted to help other kids get the chances I had been given myself. Something that goes beyond scoring a goal or lifting a trophy.

This is how (and why) my relationship with StreetFoot-ballWorld, as their ambassador, started and how eventually the idea of Common Goal would become a reality, thanks to conversations with Jürgen Griesbeck, StreetFootballWorld's founder.

The idea was 'simple': "Why don't we start something that has not been done before in football, as a team effort, and collaborate, pledging one per cent of our salaries to high-impact organisations that use football as a tool for social development? Let's try to make a first XI of players who collaborate and start from there".

Well . . . after some weeks of trying, we couldn't make the XI, but we started anyway. I pledged one per cent of my salary to the movement, and while it was a small gesture on its own, if shared, it could change the world. So, in the video of the launch, I asked my fellow professionals to join me in forming that Common Goal Starting XI, in order to create a movement based on shared values that can become integral to the whole football industry – forever.

And since then, many have joined me, from Alex Morgan to Mats Hummels, from Shinji Kagawa to Bruno Saltor and Julian Nagelsmann, the manager of RB Leizpig, from Aleksander Ceferin to FC Nordsjælland, and so many others. We have 108 members at the moment that I'm writing these lines . . . I knew I wouldn't be alone for long. I could feel that there were many people waiting for something like this: a movement that connects our beloved sport and our desire to give back.

One of the first lessons I learned in football is that it takes a team to accomplish your dreams. It's taken as an absolute truth on the pitch, and it is, and should be everywhere, but is not, certainly not in the social space.

That's the core of Common Goal: to design a collaborative way for football to give back to society. It's the most effective and sustainable way that football can deliver long-term social impact on a global scale. Football has the power to do this, but we need to act together.

The focus now is on contributions from players, but the long-term goal is to unlock one per cent of the entire football industry's revenues for grassroots football charities that strengthen their communities through sport. I believe we can do it. We have to do it, and sooner or later it will be done.

When I say that football is much more than a sport, it's because I've seen it, and not only travelling with my teams. Just a month before launching Common Goal, I travelled to Mumbai, India, to see the work of one of the organisations we collaborate with: Oscar Foundation.

After meeting the founder, Ashok Rathod, and discovering his incredible story, we went to a slum in the centre of the city, and I have to admit that at first it was very hard to comprehend the level of poverty. I remember I kept saying to myself: no child should have to live like that. Seeing the conditions, my spirits were understandably down. But then, after realising the fantastic work that the foundation was doing with the kids and the real positive impact that it was creating, I felt encouraged.

We interacted with the children, their English wasn't great, nor is my Hindi, but we communicated through laughter and football, although I'm sure most of them did not know I was a player. They might not have had many material things, but you could feel they were rich in their souls. And, I think, in the same way that I 'gave my grandfather life' – these children were giving me life.

We footballers have so many opportunities simply because we play what is essentially a children's game. I will never get tired of saying that we are so lucky to live this dream.

So I think it is fair and needed to act together and help, especially the ones who face more difficult circumstances, to have the chance to create their own destiny.

By doing so, we can show the wider professional football world that Common Goal is happening and will keep happening, because it's right. But it is everyone's responsibility to create a more just and balanced society, so I'm delighted to let you know reader, dear friend by now, that 99 per cent (one per cent seemed like very little that way, so everyone could live without it, right?) of my proceeds for this book will go to Common Goal.

Thanks for helping, thanks for reading, and see you in the next book.

**COMMON
GOAL**

With more than three billion fans, football is the largest social phenomenon on the planet. No other sport boasts such wealth. Or such reach. Or such cultural significance. The beautiful game is in a league of its own.

For many, the game forms community. It binds people together and creates a common language they can all speak. And for some, it already serves as a powerful tool for addressing social challenges in their communities. But no systematic link exists between the professional game and the many community-based football organisations around the world.

By creating a more thorough link between the players, managers, fans, organisations, brands, and 'football for good' organisations, we can join the global football community together in a team big enough and strong enough to take on the world's toughest opponents from HIV/AIDS to gender inequality to youth unemployment.

The idea is simple.

Common Goal's members pledge one per cent of their earnings to a central fund. And together we allocate this fund to high-impact organisations that harness the power of football to advance the United Nations Global Goals.

*For more information,
log on to www.common-goal.org*